Doing Conversation, Discourse and Document Analysis

Tim Rapley

SAGE

Los Angeles • London • New Delhi • Singapore

First published 2007
Reprinted 2008

SAGE Publications Ltd
1 Oliver's Yard
55 City Road
London EC1Y 1SP

SAGE Publications Inc.
2455 Teller Road
Thousand Oaks, California 91320

SAGE Publications India Pvt Ltd
B 1/I 1 Mohan Cooperative Industrial Area
Mathura Road, New Delhi 110 044
India

SAGE Publications Asia-Pacific Pte Ltd
33 Pekin Street #02-01
Far East Square
Singapore 048763

Library of Congress Control Number: 2006938289

British Library Cataloguing in Publication data

A catalogue record for this book is available from the British Library

ISBN 978-0-7619-4981-7

Typeset by C&M Digitals (P) Ltd, Chennai, India
Printed in Great Britain by The Cromwell Press Ltd, Trowbridge, Wiltshire
Printed on paper from sustainable resources

▐▌ Contents

III List of illustrations

Boxes

Figure

Editorial introduction
Uwe Flick

- Introduction to *The SAGE Qualitative Research Kit*
- What is qualitative research?
- How do we conduct qualitative research?
- Scope of *The SAGE Qualitative Research Kit*

Introduction to *The SAGE Qualitative Research Kit*

In recent years, qualitative research has enjoyed a period of unprecedented growth and diversification as it has become an established and respected research approach across a variety of disciplines and contexts. An increasing number of students, teachers and practitioners are facing questions and problems of how to do qualitative research – in general and for their specific individual purposes. To answer these questions, and to address such practical problems on a how-to-do level, is the main purpose of *The SAGE Qualitative Research Kit*.

The books in *The SAGE Qualitative Research Kit* collectively address the core issues that arise when we actually do qualitative research. Each book focuses on key methods (e.g. interviews or focus groups) or materials (e.g. visual data or discourse) that are used for studying the social world in qualitative terms. Moreover, the books in the Kit have been written with the needs of many different types of reader in mind. As such, the Kit and the individual books will be of use to a wide variety of users:

- *Practitioners* of qualitative research in the social sciences, medical research, marketing research, evaluation, organizational, business and management studies, cognitive science, etc., who face the problem of planning and conducting a specific study using qualitative methods.
- *University teachers* and lecturers in these fields using qualitative methods will be expected to use these series as a basis of their teaching.
- *Undergraduate and graduate students* of social sciences, nursing, education, psychology and other fields where qualitative methods are a (main) part of the university training including practical applications (e.g. for writing a thesis).

Each book in *The SAGE Qualitative Research Kit* has been written by a distinguished author with extensive experience in their field and in the practice with methods they write about. When reading the whole series of books from the beginning to the end, you will repeatedly come across some issues which are central to any sort of qualitative research – such as ethics, designing research or assessing quality. However, in each book such issues are addressed from the specific methodological angle of the authors and the approach they describe. Thus you may find different approaches to issues of quality or different suggestions of how to analyze qualitative data in the different books, which will combine to present a comprehensive picture of the field as a whole.

What is qualitative research?

It has become more and more difficult to find a common definition of qualitative research which is accepted by the majority of qualitative research approaches and researchers. Qualitative research is no longer just simply '*not* quantitative research', but has developed an identity (or maybe multiple identities) of its own.

Despite the multiplicity of approaches to qualitative research, some common features of qualitative research can be identified. Qualitative research is intended to approach the world 'out there' (not in specialized research settings such as laboratories) and to understand, describe and sometimes explain social phenomena 'from the inside' in a number of different ways:

- By analyzing experiences of individuals or groups. Experiences can be related to biographical life histories or to (everyday or professional) practices; they may be addressed by analyzing everyday knowledge, accounts and stories.
- By analyzing interactions and communications in the making. This can be based on observing or recording practices of interacting and communicating and analyzing this material.
- By analyzing documents (texts, images, film or music) or similar traces of experiences or interactions.

Common to such approaches is that they seek to unpick how people construct the world around them, what they are doing or what is happening to them in terms that are meaningful and that offer rich insight. Interactions and documents are seen as ways of constituting social processes and artefacts collaboratively (or conflictingly). All of these approaches represent ways of meaning, which can be reconstructed and analyzed with different qualitative methods that allow the researcher to develop (more or less generalizable) models, typologies, theories as ways of describing and explaining social (or psychological) issues.

How do we conduct qualitative research?

Can we identify common ways of doing qualitative research if we take into account that there are different theoretical, epistemological and methodological approaches to qualitative research and that the issues that are studied are very diverse as well? We can at least identify some common features of how qualitative research is done.

- Qualitative researchers are interested in accessing experiences, interactions and documents in their natural context and in a way that gives room to the particularities of them and the materials in which they are studied.
- Qualitative research refrains from setting up a well-defined concept of what is studied and from formulating hypotheses in the beginning in order to test them. Rather, concepts (or hypotheses, if they are used) are developed and refined in the process of research.
- Qualitative research starts from the idea that methods and theories should be appropriate to what is studied. If the existing methods do not fit to a concrete issue or field, they are adapted or new methods or approaches are developed.
- Researchers themselves are an important part of the research process, either in terms of their own personal presence as researchers, or in terms of their experiences in the field and with the reflexivity they bring to the role – as are members of the field under study.
- Qualitative research takes context and cases seriously for understanding an issue under study. A lot of qualitative research is based on case studies or a series of case studies, and often the case (its history and complexity) is an important context for understanding what is studied.
- A major part of qualitative research is based on text and writing – from field notes and transcripts to descriptions and interpretations and finally to the presentation of the findings and of the research as a whole. Therefore, issues of transforming complex social situations (or other materials such as images) into texts – issues of transcribing and writing in general – are major concerns of qualitative research.
- If methods are supposed to be adequate to what is under study, approaches to defining and assessing the quality of qualitative research (still) have to be discussed in specific ways that are appropriate for qualitative research and even for specific approaches in qualitative research.

Scope of *The SAGE Qualitative Research Kit*

- *Designing Qualitative Research* (Uwe Flick) gives a brief introduction to qualitative research from the point of view of how to plan and design a concrete study using qualitative research in one way or the other. It is intended to outline a framework for the other books in *The Sage Qualitative Research Kit* by focusing on how-to-do problems and on how to solve such problems in the research process. The book will address issues of constructing a research design in qualitative research; it will outline stepping-stones in making a research project work and will discuss practical problems such as resources in qualitative research but also more methodological issues like quality of qualitative research and also ethics. This framework is spelled out in more details in the other books in the *Kit*.

- Three books are devoted to collecting or producing data in qualitative research. They take up the issues briefly outlined in the first book and approach them in a much more detailed and focused way for the specific method. First, *Doing Interviews* (Steinar Kvale) addresses the theoretical, epistemological, ethical and practical issues of interviewing people about specific issues or their life history. *Doing Ethnographic and Observational Research* (Michael Angrosino) focuses on the second major approach to collecting and producing qualitative data. Here again practical issues (like selecting sites, methods of collecting data in ethnography, special problems of analyzing them) are discussed in the context of more general issues (ethics, representations, quality and adequacy of ethnography as an approach). In *Doing Focus Groups* (Rosaline Barbour) the third of the most important qualitative methods of producing data is presented. Here again we find a strong focus on how-to-do issues of sampling, designing and analyzing the data and on how to produce them in focus groups.

- Three further volumes are devoted to analyzing specific types of qualitative data. *Using Visual Data in Qualitative Research* (Marcus Banks) extends the focus to the third type of qualitative data (beyond verbal data coming from interviews and focus groups and observational data). The use of visual data has not only become a major trend in social research in general, but confronts researchers with new practical problems in using them and analyzing them and produces new ethical issues. In *Analyzing Qualitative Data* (Graham R. Gibbs), several practical approaches and issues of making sense of any sort of qualitative data are addressed. Special attention is paid to practices of coding, of comparing and of using computer-assisted qualitative data analysis. Here, the focus is on verbal data like interviews, focus groups or biographies. *Doing Conversation, Discourse and Document Analysis* (Tim Rapley) extends this focus to different types of data, relevant for analyzing discourses. Here, the focus is on existing material (like documents) and on recording everyday conversations and on finding traces of discourses. Practical issues such as generating an archive, transcribing video materials and of how to analyze discourses with such types of data are discussed.

- *Managing the Quality of Qualitative Research* (Uwe Flick) takes up the issue of quality in qualitative research, which has been briefly addressed in specific contexts in other books in the *Kit*, in a more general way. Here, quality is looked at from the angle of using or reformulating existing or defining new criteria for qualitative research. This book will examine the ongoing debates about what should count as defining 'quality' and validity in qualitative methodologies and will examine the many strategies for promoting and managing quality in qualitative research. Special attention is paid to the strategy of triangulation in qualitative research and to the use of quantitative research in the context of promoting the quality of qualitative research.

Before I go on to outline the focus of this book and its role in the *Kit*, I would like to thank some people at SAGE who were important in making this *Kit* happen. Michael Carmichael suggested this project to me some time ago and was very helpful with his suggestions in the beginning. Patrick Brindle took over and continued this support, as did Vanessa Harwoode and Jeremy Toynbee in making books out of the manuscripts we provided.

About this book
Uwe Flick

Analyzing discourse is currently one of the major approaches in qualitative research. Analyzing conversations has a long tradition in the history of qualitative research, as has the use of documents as data. In these approaches, data collection is often focused on creating a set of materials, by recording naturally occurring interactions, or selecting articles from newspapers or documents from institutional files for example. In this process, the traditional methods of data collection, which produce the data especially for the research process – as is the case in interviews or focus groups – play a minor role. Here, it is rather the ways of making available and of making up the existing materials for research purposes that are decisive. Thus, steps like the transcription of audio or video materials and the generation of an archive are core steps in the research process and not just technical or even minor issues. Ethics become relevant in this context not only in a particular but also in a different way.

This book addresses these issues from the points of view of discourse analysis and conversation analysis. In doing so, it gives topics like transcription a different and perhaps even more systematic reading than in the other books in *The SAGE Qualitative Research Kit*. Nevertheless, it is complemented by the other books in the *Kit* as well, as interviews and focus groups are special situations of conversation, which can be analyzed as such and not only for the contents that are communicated in them. Therefore, this book and the ones by Barbour (2007) on focus groups and Kvale (2007) on interviews are complementary to each other.

The same can be said for the use of visual materials (Banks, 2007), which can be used for studying discourses also. The more general approach to data analysis in Gibbs (2007) outlines ways of coding materials relevant for discourse and conversation analysis in more detail, especially concerning the use of computers and software. This book is above all devoted to a singular approach in the context of *The SAGE Qualitative Research Kit*, but at the same time it is well embedded in the more general scope of the *Kit*. The more special considerations about quality and about the planning of analysis are an addition to the more general suggestions about designing qualitative research (Flick, 2007a) and managing the quality in this process (Flick, 2007b).

▌▌▌ Acknowledgements

As this book emerges out of routine and bizarre configurations of interactions with people, texts, objects, hunches and memories, I am not quite sure who and/or what to thank. To attend to part of my dilemma I would like to paraphrase the musician Sabu Martinez: I would like to thank all those people who know me now, all those people I have known in the past but no longer see, all those people I will know in the future and all those people I will never meet.

On a more substantive note, I need to thank Uwe Flick, the series editor. Thank you for your advice, confidence and patience. Secondly, I need to shower praise on Frances Colgan, who went way beyond the identity of 'MSc student' and not only read a draft of the book but then highlighted my blatant disregard for grammar and spelling. Finally, I have to thank a whole congregation of undergraduate and postgraduate students who over the years have had to listen to me witter on about qualitative research. Generally, those teaching moments have taught me a lot.

In terms of the academy, a massive standing ovation has to go to David Silverman, who taught me what it might mean to think and write as an academic. Whilst at Goldsmiths', conversations with Ben Gidley (often over numerous large cappuccinos) helped me to begin to make sense of my work and intellectual interests. Since moving to Newcastle, Carl May has taught me what it might mean to think and write as a researcher. At Newcastle, conversations with Tiago Moreira (often over café mochas) have encouraged me to (re)think my work and interests. During my time in London (and beyond), interactions with Jon Hindmarsh, Moira Kelly, Geraldine Leydon, Annsi Peräkylä and Clive Seale have also been central. In Newcastle, working with (as well as having fun with) Ben Heaven, Neil Jenkings and Madeline Murtagh has also helped me develop my work.

As for life beyond the academy, ongoing conversations with Pete Robinson and Tom Rolands have always sharpened my thinking and often shown me how little I know. I also have to thank Adam, Andreas, Caroline, Claire, Darren, Kirsten, Laura, Liz, Graham, Matt, Micha, Rachel, Rob, Sarah, Scott, Steve and Val for listening to me ramble on about my work. BBC Radio 4 has been a constant backdrop to my thinking (as well as causing me to shout a lot at various radios I have owned) and the soundtrack for typing this book has also been supplied by the likes of Donato Wharton, Four Tet, Nick Drake and Tom McRae. I also have to thank the coffee growers, coffee beans, chocolate sauce, espresso maker and expertise of the staff at Intermezzo for supplying me with an excellent backdrop in which to consume various articles and books.

Finally, for endlessly demonstrating love, support and respect (and obviously lots of patience) and for introducing me to what it might mean to think and act with passion, intellect and wisdom, I have to thank my parents, Diane and Tony Rapley. This book is dedicated to them (and I am sure they are as surprised as I am when the boy who *hated* writing ended up doing this for a job).

1
Studying discourse

Chapter objectives
After reading this chapter, you should

- know some of the assumptions and ideas central to the study of discourse; and
- be oriented about the general outline and the purpose of the book.

Those undertaking work on conversations, discourse and documents are fascinated by language, written or spoken. I am not actually sure what those interested in discourse have not studied yet – like the Internet, nearly all the areas of human (and non-human) conduct have been investigated. There are classic pieces of work that focus on racism, sexuality and madness, but these days anything goes: from the role of 'uh huh' in talk between friends to government legislation on genetic food. The range of sources of potential materials to analyze is equally massive: official documents, statutes, political debate, all the types of media outputs, casual conversations, talk in workplaces, interviews, focus group, ethnography, Internet chat rooms, and so on. This book aims to explore how you can research language-in-use. It aims to outline in detail the very practical issues that you might face and the very practical solutions you can employ.

Some introductory thoughts

The term 'discourse analysis' is often used to describe the style of work you will see in this book. Unfortunately for you, that term has many meanings. Some people take that to mean focusing on how some specific discourses, say 'racism' and 'nationalism', are used across a range of interview transcripts or a range of newspaper editorials. Others may take it to mean focusing on how specific words, like 'the evidence suggests' or 'obviously', are used in an audiotape of a conversation or a single scientific research article to argue a specific case. Irrespective of the approach, for those analyzing discourse the primary interest is in *how language is used in certain contexts*. And the context can range from a specific moment in a conversation to a specific historical period.

On a gross level, people studying discourse see language as performative and functional: *language is never treated as a neutral, transparent, means of communication*. But rather than talk in the abstract, let me give you a 'classic' example: Two reporters see a man being shot. The next day one headline reads 'Freedom fighter kills politician' and the other headline reads 'Terrorist kills politician'. Some of the questions you could ask are:

- Which one is true?
- Which one is correct?
- Which one is factual?

And this is not just a philosophical or abstract question. We have seen this being explored in our recent history through the debates about the status of the people moved from Afghanistan to the American enclave in Cuba and interned in Guantanamo Bay. One of the debates has centred on whether these people are to be understood as 'prisoners of war' – and therefore they have specific sets of legally binding human rights – or as 'unlawful combatants'. Similarly, Pervez Musharraf, Pakistan's president, is one of many political leaders that have commented on the contemporary difficulties in defining just who is a 'freedom fighter' and who is a 'terrorist'. So as these examples begin to show, language is constructive, it is constitutive of social life. As you speak and write you produce a world.

So the interest for those analyzing discourse is on *how* language is used. The focus is on what specific version of the world, or identity, or meaning is produced by describing something in just that way over another way; what is made available and what is excluded by describing something this way over an alternative way. I can offer you another classic, albeit more mundane, example. Note that the elements of the following list are all 'true', 'correct' and/or 'facts' about me:

- I am old.
- I am young.
- I am a doctor.
- I am not a doctor.
- I was born on 10 August 1973.
- I was born on 9 August 1973.

Let us take the simplest of these contrasting statements about me – the old/young dichotomy. Well, at some moments, with some people, I get referred to as 'young'. For example, I taught some mature students and one of them entered the room late and literally refused to believe that someone my age could be the teacher; as she noted, 'I was just too young'. And it is not hard to imagine other moments when I am classified as 'old'. Am I too old to go clubbing? For me the feeling of being too old is massively dependent on such factors as the other club-bers' ages. So such categorizations can be dependent on such contextual factors as the age of the other people, the specific context or social norms.

If we think about the second pair on the list, as I work in a medical school, I am routinely reminded of my fluid and impermanent status as a 'doctor'. At var-ious moments I have been asked, 'What kind of doctor are you?' When I explain I have a PhD some people, most often medical practitioners, have been known to reply, 'So you're not a real doctor then' or 'Oh, so you're a PhD'. My mother has commented, albeit jokingly, that 'You may be a doctor, but you're not a useful one'. Also, when trying to recruit medical practitioners for research, to get access to them, I always tell the receptionist that I am 'Doctor Tim Rapley' as I know from experience that a plain 'Tim Rapley' will only get a message taken whereas the added descriptor will often get me put directly through to them. So how I choose to describe myself and how others describe me, can, and does, have effects.

Finally, the two references to my date of birth refer to two different documents that I possess. One is from my birth certificate, which offers one of the dates; I recently discovered the other date when I saw a copy of my birth record that was completed by the midwife who oversaw my delivery. As I am adopted I have no way of knowing which date is 'real'. However, the date on my birth certificate is orientated to by various institutions and institutional actors as having 'a factual status'. In terms of my passport, tax forms, insurance policies, and so on, only one of the documents, only one of the dates, is relevant. However, in terms of my per-sonal narrative, my identity as an 'adoptee', both documents are relevant. Documents produce specific realities and the realities they produce have effects.

So I can and do describe myself in a multitude of ways and others can and do describe me in different ways. I am a son, a surrogate father, an academic, a researcher, an employee, a seminar leader, a patient, and so on. The point is to focus on which description, or to put it more technically which identity, mem-bership category or subject position, among the many, is relevant, the 'work' that it does, and how that is tied to specific contexts and connects to broader culture.

Some thoughts on origins

There is no simple creation story about the birth and development of the study of discourse. Rather than see it as a single, unitary, approach to the study of language-in-use, we could see it as a field of research, a collection of vaguely related practices and related theories for analyzing talk and texts, which emerge from a diverse range of sources. It is often seen to emerge, in part, from the tradition of *social constructionism*. Vivian Burr (1995) offers four ideas that social constructionists often work with:

1   A critical stance towards taken-for-granted knowledge and understanding.
2   That our knowledge of the world is both historically and culturally specific.
3   That this knowledge is created, sustained and renewed by social processes.
4   That our knowledge and actions are intimately related and reflexively inform each other.

Put simply, our understanding of things, concepts or ideas that we might take for granted like 'sexuality', 'madness' or 'instincts' is not somehow *natural* or *pre-given* but rather is the product of human actions and interactions, human history, society and culture. For example, why should childcare responsibilities be something that is tied to specific divisions of society – most often women? Is being a parent a set of practices, skills or resources that are somehow just innate to some divisions of society and similar throughout the globe, or is it culturally and historically specific? Is being a parent somehow only a product of genetics, biology or blood or is it a set of social knowledges and actions that are practised, that we *do* parenting? Is our knowledge of being a parent something that all people just know or is this knowledge learned and generated in and through our interactions with others?

So social constructionism asks questions about everything we might take for granted – our identities, practices, knowledges and understandings. Such discussions do not necessarily have to lead us into debates about what is 'real' and what is not 'real'. As Rose notes, 'The realities that are fabricated, out of words, texts, devices, techniques, practices, subjects, objects and entities are no less real because they are constructed, for what else could they be?' (1998, p. 168). It offers us a direction of research, one in which we take seriously *how* parenting (or gender, sexuality, ethnicity, facts, truth, and so on) is produced and negotiated, the practical, active, *knowledge and action* that is engaged in as part of our everyday lives, and take seriously the *historical, social and cultural specificity* of these knowledges and actions.

The study of discourse has also been influenced by other related theories and ideas emerging from such sources as linguistics, critical psychology, deconstructionism, phenomenology, post-structuralism, postmodernism, pragmatism, and writers such as Austin, Foucault, Goffman, Garfinkel, Sacks, Schutz and Wittgenstein (to name but a few). You also have a confusing array of contemporary research traditions that focus on, at some points, the analysis of language-in-use in talk and/or texts; this includes researchers undertaking:

- Actor network theory
- Conversation analysis (which is seen by some as a 'child' of ethnomethodology)
- Ethnomethodology
- Ethnography of communication (often connected to anthropology)
- Critical discourse analysis (often connected to linguistics)
- Critical psychology
- Discursive psychology (which used to be referred to as 'discourse analysis')
- Foucauldian research (which also used to be referred to as 'discourse analysis')
- Interactional sociolinguistics
- Membership categorization analysis (which is related to both conversation analysis and ethnomethodology)
- Sociology of scientific knowledge (which is sometimes referred to as science and technology studies or social studies of science and technology).

Each tradition has its own assumptions about what counts as 'appropriate data' or 'materials' to do this type of work with and just how this type of work should be done. Also each tradition has its own terminology. For example, some people talk about 'discourses' whereas others refer to 'interpretive repertoires'; similarly some talk about 'identities', others 'subject positions', others 'categories' or even 'membership categories'.

However you conceive of its origins, the best way to get a sense of understanding what the study of discourse is about is to go and read other people's work. And unfortunately, there are no hard-and-fast rules or methods that are easily translatable into something that may look like 'a set of hard-and-fast rules or methods'. One writer describes such work as 'a craft skill, more like bike riding or sexing a chicken than following a recipe for a mild chicken rogan josh' (Potter, 1997, pp. 147–8).

Some thoughts on what is to come

This book is designed to offer you access to 'the craft skill' of collecting and working with discourse from a range of contexts and a range of perspectives. The next chapter discusses how to generate your research archive – the 'dataset' that you will find yourself working with on a day-to-day basis. I offer you a brief tour of the massive range of researchable materials that are potentially available to you. I also provide some examples of how I and other researchers found, collected and analyzed various materials. Chapter 3 then shifts to a discussion of ethics and confidentiality. I outline some general principles you should consider as well as some more detailed guidelines that may help you think about your specific research project. Thinking about the ethical implications of your research is never just a bureaucratic or organizational requirement or hurdle. It is essential that anyone who wants to conduct research has *respect* for those people they are researching and demonstrates this with their actions throughout the life of the project.

The next two chapters focus on the generation and transcription of audio and video recordings. Chapter 4 outlines the types of recording devices that are currently available. It then goes on to discuss how to recruit participants, generate research questions and record field encounters. Each of these three issues is discussed in relation to both so-called 'researcher-prompted data' – focus group or interview-based research – and so-called 'naturally occurring data' – audio- or video-based ethnographies of action and interaction. Chapter 5 then outlines different ways that you can transcribe the recordings that you generate. I use some materials that I have collected – a recording of people preparing a meal – to demonstrate some of the different ways that you can transcribe the same recording.

In Chapter 6, I then focus on how you can study talk and conversations. I show how people, mainly from the research traditions of conversation analysis and discursive psychology, work with audiotapes and videotapes of talk and interaction. Through a discussion of a range of transcripts of talk, I outline some of the key features of talk that people often focus on when analyzing conversations. The next chapter shifts to exploring how documents and texts are created, used and spoken for in various contexts. It focuses on how documents, and other 'non-human things' (like pens or computers), co-ordinate and produce people's actions and interactions. Through three case studies, I extend the prior chapter's discussion on how to study talk, and outline how a detailed analysis of moments of talk can say something about the 'big' structures and institutions of social life.

Chapter 8 outlines some of the dilemmas that you can face when you study conversations and discourse. I outline the debates around such topics as how best to understand and work with interview or focus group data; what is your role in making claims about what is going on in your data; and what can a detailed analysis of talk say about things like 'power'. Chapter 9 then focuses on the analysis of 'texts' or 'documents'. Through a range of examples and case studies, I offer you some potential ways to engage with different varieties of texts. The chapter begins with an example of a detailed analysis of a couple of lines from a newspaper dating advertisement and ends with a discussion of some documents ranging over a fifty-year period. The aim of this chapter is to give you access to a range of questions and tactics you might want to adopt when engaging with texts.

The closing chapter offers a broad overview on how to code and analyze all types of discursive materials. It draws together approaches to questioning the quality of analysis. I also outline some main 'stepping-stones' when undertaking this style of work, a list of things you may want to consider in relation to how you undertake your own work. In each chapter, the emphasis is on *the practicalities* of doing such work. I have tried to ground my discussion in a range of – hopefully interesting – empirical examples of how people have actually generated, worked on and theorized with different research materials. Importantly, in writing this book I am not seeking to offer you a set of specific criteria that 'must' be followed, but rather I have tried to suggest a range of approaches, techniques and practices that should help you begin to engage with and undertake discursive work.

≡≡≡ Key points

- Language, written or spoken, is never treated as a neutral, transparent, means of communication. Instead, language is understood as performative and functional.
- People studying discourse are interested in how language is used in certain contexts. The focus is on how specific identities, practices, knowledges or meanings are produced by describing something in just that way over another way.
- Our understanding of things, concepts or ideas that we might take for granted are not somehow natural or pre-given but rather the product of human actions and interactions, human history, society and culture.

Further reading

The following works go into more detail about the issues mentioned in this chapter:

Burr, V. (1995) *An Introduction to Social Constructionism*. London: Routledge.

Potter, J. (1996) 'Discourse analysis and constructionist approaches: theoretical background', in J. Richardson (ed.), *Handbook of Qualitative Research Methods for Psychology and the Social Sciences*. Leicester: BPS, pp. 125–40.

Wetherell, M. (2001) 'Themes in discourse research: the case of Diana', in M. Wetherell, S. Taylor and S.J. Yates (eds) *Discourse Theory and Practice: A Reader*. London: Sage, in association with The Open University, pp. 14–28.

2
Generating an archive

Chapter objectives
After reading this chapter, you should know

- how to generate your research archive – the data that you will find yourself working with on a day-to-day basis;
- about some potential sources of materials you may want to consider working with, ranging from newspaper articles to radio talk shows to video recordings of counselling sessions; and
- some examples of how I and other researchers found, collected and analyzed various materials.

The range of possible sources of material to conduct research on is massive and potentially never-ending. We now have a large range of different technologies that allow you to generate, access, store and engage with a vast array of materials. Among many things, the technologies of the printing press, camera, photocopier, tape recorder, video camera, computer and the Internet are all key to contemporary research practice. These mundane and relatively invisible technologies both enable us to conduct our research and, perhaps more importantly, now direct the focus of our research.

Sources of 'data'

To put it very simply, we could divide your possible sources of 'data' into two categories: *data that you have to generate* and *data that already exists*. By that I mean to contrast, say, a research interview you conduct on the topic of genetic disease with, say, a newspaper article on genetic disease. The newspaper article, on the face of it, exists independently of your action whereas the research interview exists only due to your action. So we could divide the potential sources of data into these two categories, *researcher-generated* and *already existing* data. However, this assumes that you are somehow more 'active' with the former category and reasonably 'passive' or 'neutral' in relation to the latter. In both cases your actions are utterly central in producing the materials as 'data'. In both cases you have to actually discover it, physically collect it, make decisions about what materials you are going to gather and what materials you are going to ignore. Irrespective of the actual form of the materials – videotapes of televisions programmes, audiotapes of focus groups, newspaper articles, screen shots of web-based discussion groups or photocopies of academic journal articles – you have made certain choices. Importantly, you have decided to call this specific ensemble of materials, which you collected together, your 'data'.

So where does that leave us? In reports of research, some things are named as 'data' and some activities are named as 'data collection'; other things and activities do not hold the same status. In one project I am working on, the two 'official' sources of data are:

- videotapes of doctor–patient consultations about a specific condition; and
- audiotapes of research interviews with patients about the consultation.

However, the findings of the research are also massively and inescapably the product of the engagement with the following materials:

- Transcripts of the doctor–patient interactions and research interviews.
- Handwritten and typed field notes of what happened prior to, during and after the consultations and interviews.
- Field notes, audiotapes and minutes of the research team's meetings and other related activities.
- Official documents distributed by the research team (including patient information leaflets, consent forms, funding documents and research reports).
- Academic research papers and books (covering such topics as social scientists writing about doctor–patient interactions; medical researchers and ethicists writing about a specific medical condition and doctor–patient interactions; and social scientific and scientific research methodology texts).
- Leaflets, handouts and newspaper cuttings (covering a specific medical condition).
- Websites (aimed specifically at social and medical researchers and the general public).
- Assorted handwritten and typed notes to myself, memos and quotes.

For me, all these materials are 'my data'. Or rather, as I prefer it, all these materials make up my archive. This archive, combined with conversations with the research team, friends, strangers, watching television, listening to the radio, reading novels, et cetera, et cetera, and most importantly, bolts from the blue (often over a large cup of coffee), enable the production of specific research findings and papers.

I could easily have called this whole section 'Generating data'. And I would have probably focused on roughly the same things. However, the scare quotes I have placed around the word 'data' may suggest I have a problem with the term. I am never quite sure when I am conducting my own research what actually *is my 'data'* and what *is not my 'data'*. Is a quote I take from a video of a doctor–patient consultation data? Whereas the quote I take from a social science article discussing doctor–patient consultations is not data? I use both to develop my argument, so for me both are data. Equally, are the topics covered in the interview data? Whereas the interview schedule itself and the reading and discussions that led to its development are somehow not data? All these areas of activity are central to producing my arguments.

Rather than just think about 'generating data', in any narrow sense, *you to need to think about generating or producing an archive – a diverse collection of materials that enable you to engage with and think about the specific research problem or questions*. On a practical level, this means collecting and managing an array of different materials. And obviously, what materials make up your archive is directed by *both* your specific research question and your theoretical trajectory. In order to briefly review the possible sources of researchable materials, I am going to divide the following discussion into two areas: *document-based sources* and *audio- and visual-based sources*. I should note that this is a wholly arbitrary division. For example, when an audiotape is transcribed it is, in one sense, translated into a document. However, this arbitrary or working division is just that, is based on my need to offer you a relatively accessible and manageable story.

Document-based sources

On the face of it, this would appear the easier archive to generate. And to be honest, it can be. As a lot of the material you could be working on will already be in the 'public domain' – either published on paper or on the web – you do not have to go through the process of getting consent to use the material or recruiting and recording often very busy people. Your major considerations are often related to how to initially *discover*, then *source,* and then make some form of *recording* of the documents. In this section, I am just going to offer a few examples of documents you could use and talk about some of the general pitfalls and problems. In Chapter 9, I shall offer some more detailed cases.

The most ubiquitous and accessible source of documents are *newspaper and magazine articles*. This is a *massive* potential resource for most academic projects. You only have to think about the diversity of weekly and daily local and national newspapers, as well as the ever-growing numbers of general and specialist magazines we are confronted with on a day-to-day basis, to realize how much material is easily available for analysis. You can learn a lot about the directions and trajectory of culture and institutional practice in and through engaging with these materials.

Let us take, for example, a recent phenomenon – articles and magazines specifically targeted at men and their relationship with their bodies. When you look at the cover of a monthly magazine like *Men's Health* you will be witnessing specific discourses of masculinity. Each cover seems to have headlines like 'how to tone your stomach in one month' or 'six exercises to develop a six pack', alongside pictures of men with washboard stomachs. This raises various questions, including: What (new) versions of masculinity are being promoted? What (new) connections are men meant to make between their bodies and self-identity? Are men (now) objects of a female gaze? I hope it is easy to see how an analysis of such headlines, and the articles that they refer to, might raise some very interesting questions about new formations of masculinity.

Research has also focused solely on *newspaper headlines*; for example, Lee (1984) offers a wonderful analysis of the headline 'Girl Guide Aged 14 Raped At Hell's Angels Convention'. Among many things, he highlights how this headline works to attract our attention and persuade us to engage with that story. The headline raises a puzzle: how is it that these two categories of people – 'Girl Guides' and 'Hell's Angels' – not routinely connected, are together? How is it that they were in the same space? And this is not *any* space, this is a specific type of space with specific un-Girl-Guide-like associations and activities, this is a 'Hell's Angels Convention'. In part, we may engage with this story to find a solution to this puzzle. That we engage with this *as* a potential puzzle in search of potential solutions, is intimately dependent on some shared understanding of culture and cultural categories. Research has also focused on the text (and images) in such things as *advertisements, magazine front covers, dating or 'would like to meet' adverts*, as well as the actual *magazine articles* and *newspaper reports*.

So work has ranged from focusing on a single headline, a single article or a single publication to a very large number of *national and international newspaper publications*. With studies that work with a larger archive, you obviously somehow have to make your archive *manageable*. For example, Seale (2002) studied how cancer is portrayed in regional and national newspapers across different cultures. His archive was based on one week's newspaper publications from the English-language press all over the world that contained the words 'cancer' and 'leukaemia' or 'leukemia'. His choice to concentrate on just one week's press was driven by various practical concerns, including generating a manageable number of articles (his initial search generated 2,419 English-language articles) and the actual cost of conducting and gathering this amount of material (he went through a specialized company that collates and compiles the material for you and e-mails it to you). He only worked on articles written in English due to the cost of and potential problems with translation. You need to be aware that simply finding, collecting, sifting through and then physically and/or electronically working with a large number of articles can take large amounts of time and money.

Another massive potential source of documents for research are *academic publications*. These can range from publications in the areas of the sciences, medicine, the arts and humanities and the social sciences and can be either more historical or more contemporary documents. Obviously, the term 'historical' is contingent, and can refer to anything from documents produced ten years ago to, say, three hundred years ago (and many, many more). A lot of contemporary work is focused on analyzing the vast array of contemporary or historical academic articles and books of other researchers. Much of this work rarely offers a novice reader any hint as to how the materials included were discovered or selected (or even analyzed).

As with much research work, analyzing academic publications involves a lot of common-sense practices and some related detective work. Emerging from some research I was doing on how social researchers conduct unstructured interviews, drawing on audiotapes of actual interviews, I wanted to discover what researchers are told interviewing should look like, what prescriptions of ideal interviewer practice were being promoted. I felt this was important as qualitative or in-depth interviewing had become the method of choice in the social sciences, especially in sociology, and so a vast array of literature on 'how to be a good interviewer' existed. I already knew of some of the key or landmark texts to focus on. In part this was because these were the articles and books that 'everybody' seemed to reference when discussing or justifying their choice of using qualitative interviews. I went to these articles and books and looked at their reference lists and followed the trail back. I then found these articles and repeated the process. It is a hit-and-miss affair; some articles were highly relevant whilst others were utterly redundant. I also conducted some computer-based literature searches, looking for the much more recent literature on qualitative interview methods. I found and read the more 'basic' how-to methods texts (much like this one) and the more 'scholarly' philosophical and methodological debates. I also gathered a collection of research articles that used qualitative interviews as a method.

In the end, I had a massive pile of photocopied articles and chapters, a large collection of library books (and library fines). During all this time, I tried to arrange the debates that emerged in these texts into some kind of order: to trace the patterns and similarities as well as to spot the moments of disjuncture. In my initial period of generating my archive, I was overwhelmed; it was tricky to form a reasoned division between the different texts I was reading. Over time, it became much easier as I developed a sense of the different discourses on 'how to be a good interviewer'. After several failed attempts, I finally developed a typology of the different methodological prescriptions that was both coherent and, most importantly, reflected the materials in my archive.

A further source of materials are *government publications and parliamentary debates*. Most governments produce a large number of publications, which are often available for free over the Internet. They routinely outline directions of future policy and/or strategy and in so doing review contemporary debates and research on specific issues. These documents are often a wonderful source to discover and map specific discourses, especially as they document past and forthcoming (or foreshadow potential) changes in the legislation and/or the organization of society and social institutions. In the UK, the debates in the House of Commons and House of Lords are all recorded in a massive series of books called *Hansard*. You can trace the trajectory of debates from the legalization of cannabis to the Sexual Discrimination Act. As these are all *public documents*, in that anyone can have access to them, your immediate concerns are centred on getting *physical access* to them and then being able to navigate through the vast quantity of materials.

In the UK, you can also get access to some of the *private documents* of governmental departments, those documents not initially deemed for external consumption. These can include letters or memos between civil servants in government departments, between civil servants and various non-governmental experts or organizations, as well as international correspondence. For example, Gidley (2003) used documents from the The National Archives in London to help him explore the experience of East London Jewish Radicals in the early twentieth century. As individuals in these groups were closely monitored by the British police and other government departments, he found a wealth of material including police-made transcriptions of anti-war meetings and reports of the various venues they congregated in. Through engaging with this archive, he not only discovered something about the radical groups themselves but also a history of the policing and governing of these communities.

As with government-based documents, you can generally get access to *nongovernmental organizations', corporations', charities' and institutions' public documentation*. Most organizations have some form of public face or public documentation, ranging from promotional leaflets to press releases and company reports. Again, these enable you to engage with and trace specific fields and trajectories. If your focus was on the various discourses surrounding smoking, you may search for leaflets and literature from anti- and pro-smoking charities, reports from the governing bodies of medical professions and press releases from tobacco manufacturers. Obviously, these sources may make up only part of your archive. But given the growth of the Internet – and most organizations now have a web-based presence – your ability to easily access such potentially useful material has massively increased. Getting access to these types of organizations' private, internal or in-house documents – their 'behind the scenes' persona – is often extremely difficult and usually involves either already knowing someone on the inside, sheer persistence, or just plain luck. In the UK, the introduction of the Freedom of Information Act may change this, as you can now request information from companies that is not deemed 'commercially sensitive'.

Sources that are routinely massively under used by many social scientists are *diaries, biographies, literature and poetry*. Obviously, diaries and biographies, given their apparently more factual status than literature, clearly offer us access to whatever period or practice the person is describing. Generally, unless the subject is reasonably famous (for whatever reason) and therefore these diaries are actually published, just being aware of their existence can be problematic. In recent years *blogs,* or *web-based diaries,* have grown rapidly. They can be a fascinating and easily accessible source of both descriptions of mundane, routine, everyday activities and experiences as well as more esoteric practices and political standpoints. Alongside this, literature and poetry, albeit often named as fiction, can beautifully document historical and contemporary social and cultural ideas and practices. For example, contemporary 'chick lit' fiction nicely documents a range of versions of femininity (and masculinity). Such fictional accounts are never irrelevant or outside our social worlds but rather offer another way to reflect on a specific topic or idea.

A final source of potential materials, as I have outlined repeatedly above, is the *Internet*. It is useful not only as a space through which you gain access to specific documents, or screen shots of web pages, but also due to the specific Internet-based media of communication, including *e-mails, news groups* and *bulletin boards*. If you ever want to use these sources, you should seriously consider whether you should ask the participants for permission to quote from them. Some academic news groups I belong to do not support *any* of the postings being used as research material.

Some practical considerations when working on documents

Getting *physical access* to documents is important. One of the obvious starting places is to search on the Internet. You can often find some of the documents you need, or at the very least learn where you need to go to find them. There are now many web-based directories of libraries, detailing the range of their holdings as well as the catalogues of more specialized libraries. Some of these specialized libraries' material might be available online.

Another solution is your nearest university or public library. You often find that they do not have exactly what you need. You then need to discover if this material can be ordered in from another library. This not always a satisfactory solution, as some libraries will put restrictions on the number of documents you can request at any one time or you may not be able to order some of the material at all. Also, a lot of the time you may not know whether that article, that book or that magazine you have ordered is something you really need until you actually get to read it.

If your research is reasonably specialized, or is focused on historical documents, you will probably have to visit specialized libraries (often known as archives). In the UK, examples of these archives include The National Archives (official archive of the UK Government), The Women's Library and the National Film and TV Archive. Some libraries' collections have restricted access, which may mean you need to get some form of special permission to visit them. This permission can range from a letter from your supervisor or university to becoming an (honorary) member of that institution. Others may have open access. In the majority of the cases you will have to visit such specialist libraries in person.

You may also have *restricted access* to documents in other ways:

- Although a huge volume of government documents are released and available for public scrutiny, some files are 'closed'. This is especially the case with military and espionage reports, where documents may be closed and then only released into the public domain after a set number of years. And even when they are 'opened', some of the words may be obscured, some pages or whole files removed.
- When documents have been produced for 'internal' consumption in an organization or between individuals, you will generally have some problems getting access to them. You may even have problems finding out that they exist at all! Obviously, to get access to such documents you will have to negotiate with the specific organization or individuals you are working with.
- Depending on your topical focus, you may end up working with some documents that employ very technical or specialized language, abbreviations or conventions. However, during the course of your research, as you become more submerged in your field, you should hopefully become more familiar with the language that those already members of the area take for granted. In such cases, it may be possible to use a 'technical' dictionary to initially help you, or you may have access to an insider to provide relevant translations. Also, reading other accounts of the area, often written by other social scientists, can help you learn about the forms and routines of the language.
- In some areas you will discover that a potential key document, or series of documents, will be written in a language you cannot read. You will need to search for an appropriate translation or ask about amongst your colleagues or friends to see if they can translate (part of) it for you. Prior to paying someone to translate a whole document – which is quite expensive – you really need to check whether that document will be central and what level of detail you need to work with. Do you need a word-for-word translation, will a brief summary suffice, or do you only need specific parts translated?

As you will (hopefully) be working quite closely on the documents, you really need copies of the original documents. When working with documents from libraries, as well as internal organizational documents, you will often not be allowed to take the original documents away from the building. With some documents, often due to age (and within organizations, potential sensitivity), you may not be able to photocopy *any* of the documents and so will only be able to make notes. Bear in mind you can only take so many notes or do so much verbatim copy by hand (or preferably onto a laptop computer) in any one visit. Also, some libraries may have restrictions on both the number of documents you can request on each visit as well as the number of documents you can photocopy at any one time.

A final point is to remember to take detailed notes of where that document (or that specific quote) came from, *whilst you are actually collecting the documents*. Despite my good intentions, whilst writing up I usually find at least one document or quote that I have absolutely no idea where I got it from or have any references for. Please try not to echo my mistake.

Some closing comments on working with documents

In general, you work with a range of documents, covering both:

- *primary sources*: historically contemporary and/or first-hand accounts; and
- *secondary sources*: historically or spatially distant and/or second-hand accounts.

For example, I became interested in why, when we visit the theatre, we all sit very quietly, become relatively immobile and condemn others (and sometimes feel anger towards others) for breaching these rules. I went to various archives and generated a collection of materials on and around the audience in London's theatres. I learned that it is only in the recent past, over a period between the nineteenth and twentieth centuries, especially around the 1880s, that theatre-goers became increasingly 'tamed'. Prior to this, audiences did things like shout at actors to repeat what they felt were well-delivered monologues, talked to their friends who had purchased the more expensive seats that were placed on stage, or threw food at actors who they felt were 'bad'. The shift from the more carnivalesque occurrences of past audiences to today's docile assembly was mediated by various trajectories, including:

- the growth of a new middle class (with new 'polite' values and norms);
- the introduction of gas stage lighting (with the audience now sitting in darkness); and
- the entrepreneurship of certain theatre owners (with the building and refurbishment of theatres to cater for the new, refined, middle classes).

This research was made possible by using secondary sources – more 'academic' books and articles on the history of theatrical performance, design, production and ownership – *and* primary sources, such as nineteenth-century critics' commentaries on certain productions and audience behaviour, actors and audience members' diaries and letters, newspaper articles, debates in Parliament and theatrical trade publications.

Often the best starting point *is to read other academic work on the specific topic and to find out what documents they used and where they found them.* These secondary sources will generally provide commentaries on and copies of (parts of) the original documents and may contain the details of the specific places they sourced the original documents from. Generally, you will want to focus your analysis on these or other original documents, on primary sources, rather than just rely on these secondary accounts.

Even if your research is not primarily focused on how the press, academics, individuals or organizations render knowledge about your specific topic, or you are not really interested in tracing the history and development of ideas, practices or institutions that we take for granted today, documents about that topic can help you engage with and re-think about the research. They are vital resources for any form of research, be it as part of the stages or practices called 'literature reviews', 'background reading' or 'producing questions for focus groups' or as ways to spark new (and old, long forgotten) thoughts about your research. As such, being aware of and engaged with text-based documents is essential to *all* research practice. The other key source in contemporary research practice is audio- and visual-based sources. It is to these that we now turn.

Audio- and visual-based sources

As with documents, you have a wide and ever-growing variety of potential sources to work with. With document-based research you are working with materials that already exist, often in a published form; your major issue is generally just getting access to them. When working with audio- and visual-based sources some of these materials already exist, like television programmes, whereas with others you have to take some part in generating them, like interviews or videos of interactions.

There are various sources to work with; for example, some people work with recordings of all types of *radio and television programmes.* A lot of work has been undertaken on *news interviews,* both radio and television based. Heritage and Greatbatch (1991) have used audio and video recordings of the news to understand the interactional work that occurs between the news interviewer and their interviewees. For example, rather than say something like 'You're an idiot', news interviewers routinely say something like 'Mr Smith says you're idiot' or 'Some people say you're an idiot'. This is just one of the practices that locally produces the 'impartiality' or 'objectivity' of news interviewing and so sustains the impartial status of the institution of news interviews. This style of work involves a very detailed focus on the interactional work of the speakers – the *form* of the talk – and is often less concerned with the specific topic that is actually being talked about on the programme. Williams et al. (2003) take a different approach, where the actual *content* of the talk was the focus. They were concerned to understand how information about embryonic stem cell research was portrayed throughout the news media. They used recordings of TV news reporting, focusing on the *televised debates,* alongside newspaper articles to outline how the ethical arguments of those for and against stem cell research were covered by the media.

Researchers have also analyzed *documentaries*, focusing on how the programme works to produce its specific account as 'factual' and/or 'objective', alongside exploring what specific version of the world the documentary outlines. Others have focused on *radio talk-shows*. Some research has focused more on the content of these phone-in programmes, the specific topics covered or the debates. Others, like Hutchby (1996), focused more on the form of such programmes. He outlined how the hosts of these programmes work to encourage debate: rather than remaining neutral, they routinely take the opposite point of view of the caller and so encourage argumentative talk, as well as sometimes openly agreeing with the caller's perspective.

Whatever approach has been taken, all these researchers had to generate their own specific archives of materials. Some of them obtained the recordings of specific programmes from another archive that already existed. For example, Williams et al. (2003) had access to an archive that contained all the main TV bulletins and UK national newspaper articles that focused on human genetics research in the year 2000. In this case, someone had already collected all the relevant (national) material for them and so their analysis was based on a subsample of that archive. All they had to do was search through that archive to find all the materials that referred to stem cell research. In general, you will not always be that fortunate. Such comprehensive archives may not exist for your specific topic area. However, in saying that, it is always worth checking out if any do exist. They may be held by specific academics, academic departments or specialized libraries.

More routinely, you will have to start from scratch and actually discover and record your own material. Recording, then, can often be relatively easy, as all you need is either a television and video recorder or a radio and audio recorder. You may also find that the audiovisual department of a university (with enough notice and appropriate paperwork) has the facilities to record programmes for you. Also, if for whatever reason you forgot or failed to record a specific programme, you could always try and contact the radio or television company that originally broadcast the programme; they may, if you explain your research interest, provide you with a copy. Similarly, many radio programmes are now archived on the Internet, so you may be able to download them from there. Whatever you do, *please be aware of how copyright law works in your country*. If you want to reproduce a still image from a television programme in a journal article, it is more than likely that you will have to seek the permission of the owner of the copyright of that image. That may mean contacting the company that broadcast the programme or the actual production company.

As with document-based materials, you could also focus on fictional radio and television programmes, be they *soap operas, drama serials, plays or films*. Again, albeit often under the title of cultural studies, a huge body of work focuses on how specific themes or ideas are explored and portrayed in fictional media. For example, next time you watch a romantic comedy, think about how certain versions of gender are situated, sustained and (occasionally) subverted and how they routinely produce heterosexual relationships as the *only* form of relationship. Similarly, how do the contemporary *Star Trek* programmes offer a specific moral and ethical version of the human practice? How are the debates around the role of biotechnology and the fear of the cyborg echoed and explored in these series? Television and radio programmes offer us access to a wealth of potentially researchable materials as they offer access to materials that focus on, describe and render (nearly) all activities and forms of life.

Other researchers work with recordings of *interviews and focus groups* (see Barbour, 2007; Kvale, 2007). Routinely, discursive work on these types of data has focused more on the content of the talk. For example, Edley and Wetherell (1997) used interviews with small groups of teenage boys to focus on how they talked about their own gender identities. They noted how their interviewees produced plural and often conflicting versions of masculinity, how they worked to distance themselves from being understood as 'macho men' or 'wimps'. They sought to produce themselves as 'new men', but in so doing, this new identity was still based on the values of 'machoness'.

The call for 'naturally occurring' data

Schegloff (1999) offers the following story about an aphasiologist (someone who deals with speech disorders caused by dysfunction of the language areas of the brain):

> (W)hile engaged in testing aphasic patients, he would ordinarily use rest periods during which patients had a coffee to go and check his mail, etc. One day he happened to join the patients in the coffee room during the break and was astonished to hear the patients doing things while talking amongst themselves or with relatives which they had just shown themselves to be 'unable' to do in the preceding test session (1999, p. 431)

This story nicely demonstrates the potential benefits of *a focus on what people do in the context of their everyday lives.* By using audio and video recordings and observations of 'naturally occurring' interactions over interviews, or experiments, or imagining you already know, you can gain a different perspective on people's actions and interactions.

Recently, there has been a turn away from relying solely on interview- or focus-group-based data. The problem for some researchers is that with this type of data you are relying solely on participants' self-reports or accounts of what they do. As Strong (1980) notes, just prior to his incredibly insightful analysis of interviews with doctors about their treatment of alcoholic patients:

> One further aside. No form of interview study, however devious or informal, can stand as an adequate substitute for observational data. The inferences about actual practice that I or others may draw from those interviews are therefore somewhat illegitimate. My excuses must be that at present we have no better data on the treatment of alcoholic patients and that, more generally, I have at least attempted to ground myself as fully as possible in these few observational studies of medical consultations that have so far been undertaken. Whether all this is a sufficient guide to the specific matter of practice with alcoholics must remain an open question for the moment. (1980, pp. 27–8)

I am inclined to agree with Strong's version. For me, an interview or focus group study that *only* uses participants' accounts to understand people's day-to-day practices seems problematic.

The interview or focus group may be an economical means, in the sense of time and money, of getting access to an 'issue'. It may also be an economical means of getting access to issues that are not easily available for analysis, to get people to 'think out loud' about certain topics. However, having said this, most topics are 'freely available' for analysis. As Holstein and Gubrium (1995) note, to understand the topic 'family' we do not *need* to interview people or enter people's homes. We can see *how* 'family' is organized, produced and negotiated on the bus, in supermarkets, in newspapers, in talk-shows, in legislation, and so on. The point is, whether it is an interview, a focus group, or an observation of an office or supermarket, *you should be sensitive that people's actions and interactions are contextually situated.* By contextually situated I simply mean that we massively shape our actions and interactions to 'fit with' (and so reproduce) the, often unspoken, norms, rules and expectations of the specific context we find ourselves in. You only have to think of how you behave differently in a church or classroom from in a pub or at a friend's house, or how you recount the same story in different ways to different friends or different members of your family, to get a sense of what contextually situated might mean. Also, you just know at a glance when someone is behaving 'oddly' in a situation; this sense of oddness may in part emerge from their breaching the expectations of what is appropriate conduct for that context.

It is important to note what people mean when they say that they prefer to focus on 'naturally occurring' interaction. Some people take it to mean that you should only use data that is *not* researcher-led or researcher-prompted. With this reading you would not be interested in working with interview or focus group data but rather only be interested in recording and analyzing occasions that would take place if you were not present. With this line of argument the Holy Grail is to use only video and audio data that is (reasonably) untainted by any researcher's actions. Short of using hidden cameras or microphones and never being present at the scene, this is an impossible dream; as numerous studies of interaction have shown, the emergent properties of an encounter are intimately related to a whole range of facets of that scene and this includes the presence of 'silent witnesses', like researchers, cameras or microphones.

However, what I take a focus on naturally occurring activity to mean is that you should *try to discover how some action or interaction* – be it a police interrogation or a qualitative interview – *occurs as 'natural', normal or routine.* So, rather than only asking a focus group moderator about how they run focus groups, you can gain a good understanding of 'how they run focus groups' through some form of recordings of them actually running focus groups. Equally, rather than asking counsellors about how they counsel, you may want to base many of your observations on recordings of them actually doing some counselling. From this perspective, researcher-led information – from interviews or other sources – is still of use in trying to describe how counsellors do counselling, or how focus group moderators run focus groups. However, the primary source of data would often be audio or video recordings of what they actually do as they do it. When analyzing both the videotapes of counsellors in action and the interviews with them about their specific practice, you would obviously take into account how your actions and any recording equipment impacted on the ongoing encounters.

So the call for naturally occurring interaction in this sense means that, no matter what sources of data you are relying on, your main interest would be generating a sense of *how the specific thing you are interested in routinely occurs or 'comes off' as it does.* As such, researchers interested in these types of studies have focused on a vast range of practices, from how Tibetan monks discuss logic, how neurobiologists dissect rats, how qualitative interviewers ask questions and listen to interviewees' answers, to how people disagree when talking to friends. All this work is, at the very least, based around observations and/or audio or video recordings of these practices as they occur. And in the chapters that follow, I will further unpack how to generate and work with audio- and video-based data.

21

Some closing comments

Hopefully you have gained just a few ideas about the potential sources of materials you could work with and are not too overwhelmed by the sheer number of options you have available to you. Ideally, what you need to do is get a very general sense of what the focus of your research is, what approach you are going to take, and therefore you will be in a position to make a decision about what materials you are going to generate your findings and conclusions on.

▤ Key points

- You should generate an archive – a diverse collection of materials that enable you to engage with and think about the specific research problem or questions. Your archive could contain document-based sources as well as audio- and visual-based sources.
- Read other academic work on your specific topic and find out what research materials they used and how they collected them.
- Rather than solely relying on researcher-initiated audio- and visual-based materials, for example, interviews or focus groups, some academics argue that you should focus on 'naturally occurring' data.

Further reading

These sources explore in a little more detail the methods I addressed in this chapter:

Barbour, R. (2007) *Doing Focus Groups* (Book 4 of *The SAGE Qualitative Research Kit*). London: Sage.

Gidley, B. (2004) 'Doing historical and archival research', in C. Seale (ed.), *Researching Society and Culture* (2nd edn). London: Sage, pp. 249–64.

Kvale, S. (2007) *Doing Interviews* (Book 2 of *The SAGE Qualitative Research Kit*). London: Sage.

Scott, J. (1990) *A Matter of Record: Documentary Sources in Social Research*, Cambridge: Polity Press.

Taylor, S. (2001a) 'Locating and conducting discourse analytic research', in M. Wetherell, S. Taylor and S.J. Yates (eds), *Discourse as Data: A Guide for Analysis*. London: Sage, in association with The Open University, pp. 5–48.

3
Ethics and recording 'data'

Chapter objectives
After reading this chapter, you should

- know some general principles you should consider as well as some more detailed guidelines that may help you think about your specific research project; and
- be aware that anyone who wants to conduct research has respect for those people they are researching and demonstrates this with their actions throughout the life of the project.

Prior to recording *any* data, you have to consider the *ethical implications* of your research. In recent years there has been a growth in concern over the ethical obligations of researchers. There has been a shift from describing those who take part in research as 'research subjects' to *research participants*. This shift in language demonstrates the concern for the rights of the participants as well as an awareness that the research process can, potentially, adversely affect those who take part. Various professional associations, for example the British Sociological Association and the American Psychological Association, as well as many university departments or research centres now have their own code of ethics and/or detailed recommendations about what constitutes appropriate conduct (see also Flick, 2007a, chap. 7).

In general terms, you should be aware of the relevant guidelines, recommendations or codes of ethical conduct that could apply to the research you undertake. In most countries,

- health-related research,
- research with the vulnerable (e.g. legal minors, people with mental disabilities) and
- research covering sensitive or emotive topics (e.g. child abuse, termination)

require a greater level of official ratification and/or care. For example, in the UK, when researching National Health Service patients or members of staff (whether surgeons, managers or janitors), researchers have to submit a detailed proposal to an appropriate research ethics committee in order to gain access to the field. You should also be aware that universities have ethics committees and that you may be required, either as a student or a member of staff, to submit a project proposal prior to beginning any fieldwork. You may also have to consider specific *legal obligations*; for example, in the UK access to patient medical records is strictly protected and governed. With broadcast media, such as recordings of television or radio programmes, you may have to get written permission from a specific broadcaster to reproduce images of the programme.

Above all, your research *should not cause any harm or distress, either psychological or physical, to anyone taking part in it.* And this refers to both the time during the fieldwork, when you may have contact with the participants, as well as when you write up the research, when (hopefully) the work is published. Secondly, anyone taking part in the research *should be aware that they are taking part in research, understand what the research is about and consent to take part in it.* This means that you should *not* be conducting covert or undercover research, that you should *not* secretly video or audio-record people. Researchers in the past have undertaken covert recordings, for example making hidden recordings of conversations with far-right militia or racist groups, where identifying themselves as researchers could lead to violence. I would never advise anyone to do this type of research *as you should never place yourself in any dangerous situation* and also because you can conduct such research overtly; some representatives of these groups will probably talk to you or you could work on other sources of data, say their printed or web-based publications.

I am now just going to outline some general principles you should consider and some more detailed guidelines that may help you think about your specific research project. I should note that most of what I say applies to audio and video recordings and photographs that you or others make on your behalf. This covers things like interviews (see Kvale, 2007), focus groups (see Barbour, 2007) that you have arranged and may well be an active participant in, as well as encounters you are observing or recording (see Angrosino, 2007), such as counselling sessions, company meetings or interactions in classrooms. Different considerations and regulations can apply to recordings in public spaces and I highlight these at the end of the section.

I should note that the guidelines offered in the following section may appear relatively daunting. Don't panic. The majority of the recommendations given below are very easily fulfilled. If you have a good set of ideas to explore, on a topic that is relevant with a design that is do-able, you should have little problem. Most people are very happy to take part in research.

Some ethical issues on making and recording research 'data'

In this section I am going to draw on some guidelines drawn up by the United Kingdom General Medical Council (2002) as they offer a useful range of points for us to consider. I want to stress that you should use these to *reflect on* your specific research project; they are in no way exhaustive or definitive. Whether you undertake a specific action will depend entirely upon the specific auspices of your project.

The first two guidelines, on the face of it, seem fairly self-explanatory:

- Seek permission to make the recording and get consent for any use or disclosure.
- Give participants adequate information about the purpose of the recording when seeking their permission.

Prior to making any recording you should ask the participants whether they will allow you to make that recording. However, it is not good enough to turn up at the research site, start unpacking your video recorder and tripod, and then say 'Hey, by the way, can I record this?' You need to gain something that is called *informed consent*. Ideally, you need to give the participants enough information about the nature and purpose of the research (and what you are actually going to do with the recordings you collect) for them to be able to make an informed choice about whether or not to take part. In practice, what actually constitutes 'adequate information' is not always a clear-cut process. I want to give you two examples of how I gained informed consent, one of them being a lot more rigorous than the other (see Boxes 3.1 and 3.2).

Box 3.1   Example 1: Interviews with managers in the construction industry about women's roles

With this project I recruited interviewees over the phone. During this initial phone call, I explained the outline of the project: that we were doing research on women's involvement in the construction industry; that I wanted to interview them about their company's current employment practices with regard to women; and who funded our research. If they agreed to the interview, I then arranged a suitable date and time to visit them and also asked them whether I could audiotape the interview. No one refused for the interview to be recorded. When I turned up on the day of the interview, I asked them if they had any further questions about the research project and whether it was still all right for me to tape-record the interview. A lot of the interviewees asked me what was going to happen to the research, so I explained that we would be

(Continued)

---

writing a report for our funding body and then publishing the research in academic journals. I also offered the interviewees copies of our final report.

Box 3.2 Example 2: Interviews and focus groups with general practitioners about patients with alcohol problems

Initially, general practitioners and patients were recruited via letters. We sent them all a covering letter briefly outlining the remit of the project, an information sheet and a consent form. The information sheet was roughly two sides of A4. The opening section offered the following overview of the aims of project.

What is the purpose of the study?

Alcohol-related problems cause management difficulties for many GPs. It is now well established that:

- There is good research evidence that certain interventions can reduce alcohol-related problems.
- That GPs believe this work is important, but often believe patients are unwilling to change their behaviour.
- That a variety of social factors cause GPs to be selective about the kinds of patients they intervene with.

We aim to identify and describe the *clinical* and *social* factors that regulate the discussion of alcohol-related problems, and how they promote or inhibit effective engagement with this group of patients.

Through one-to-one qualitative interviews, we want to explore your experiences of the detection and management of alcohol-related problems in the primary care consultation. We then want to follow up the findings of these individual discussions with group interviews.

This information sheet also covered such details as:

- Where and when the interviews will take place.
- What the discussions will involve.
- What we will do with the recordings and transcripts.
- The potential benefits and disadvantages of taking part.
- What we are going to do with the results.
- Who is funding the research.
- Contact details for further information.

(Continued)

(Continued)

If they agreed to take part in the project they either filled in and signed the consent form and sent it by post or when I arrived at the interview they either handed me a completed form or they completed the form in front of me. The consent form is outlined below:

CONSENT FORM
Negotiating alcohol problems in the primary care consultation

Please tick
the box if
you agree

I agree to take part in the one-to-one interview for the 'Negotiating alcohol problems in the primary care consultation' study. ☐

I agree to take part in the group interview for the 'Negotiating alcohol problems in the primary care consultation' study. ☐

I agree to the interviews being tape-recorded and transcribed and understand that the recordings and transcripts will be treated as confidential and securely stored at all times and that only members of the research team will have access to them. I also understand that the original recordings will be destroyed within six weeks of transcription. ☐

I understand that I am free to withdraw from the study at any time without having to give any reason. ☐

Name: ———————————————— Date: —————
(Please print)

Signature: ————————————————

Immediately prior to the interview I asked if they had any further questions about the project and many of the interviewees asked me quite detailed questions.

As these examples show, for each project, you do not have to explain your key theoretical assumptions or the mechanics of how you will analyze the data. I should note that the amount of detail you offer will vary from participant to participant. Above all, the information sheet should be written in a *clear and accessible style* – without academic jargon or shorthand.

With hindsight, I would never repeat the practices of the Women in Construction project. In today's legalistic environment it is *essential* to get participants to sign a consent form. I also feel that providing an information sheet is not only central to ethical research practice but also potentially useful to your project. It is central as the potential participant has the opportunity to consider the project in their own time. If they have some form of text available to them, either on a screen or on paper, it can enhance their ability to reflect on the implications of their possible involvement and can also be used in any discussion they have with other people (managers, colleagues, friends, etc.), in that they too can read the document. It can be useful in some diverse ways, for example:

- In producing the document you are forced to re-think the project. Being asked to explain it in a clear and accessible way can make you reflect on the topic, the research design and why your research is important.
- It may offer a professional identity or legitimacy to the project and so may influence people's willingness to take part.
- The potential participants can 'think with' the document and this can lead them to ask some interesting questions or make some thought-provoking observations about the research. These can become a really useful source of additional 'data' or further research questions or make you rewrite the information sheet, as you discover that certain parts are unclear.

Prior to starting the recording, you may want to deliberately encourage participants to talk about some of the ideas on the information sheet. In this way it can become a more active, informative, document rather than just a token gesture towards ethical practice. By inciting the participant to speak about the ideas or information in the document, such as through asking them to raise any specific questions or concerns or just talking through one of the sections, they may begin to demonstrate whether they actually do or do not comprehend what is involved. Sometimes participants say 'It's all quite clear' and then you discover that they had just agreed 'because it's from the university' or hoped that something that was unclear would become clear during the recording process.

One of the assumptions of gaining informed consent is that *the participant must have the ability to comprehend the implications of them giving their permission*. Certain groups in our society are not seen as autonomous, that is, they are without the ability to self-govern, as they lack a 'full capacity' to understand. These groups include *children* (in the UK, those under sixteen) and *people with certain mental impairments* or *people with mental illness* (for example, Alzheimer's disease or schizophrenia). Importantly, with these groups you *must* get permission from a legal guardian (often a parent) or a close relative or carer. With most of the participants in these groups, for example, children of school age, you should seek permission from both the children's parents or guardians *and* the children themselves. When working with such potentially powerless and disadvantaged groups, it is always best to seek additional advice from experts or expert groups in the area or from university research ethics committees.

Finally, with some research projects, say a study of day-to-day work practices in a restaurant or a printing firm, you may be asked to visit the site and give a small presentation to all the staff. In this way, you will not only be outlining the remit of the project and answering any questions but also starting the process of enabling informed consent.

We now need to consider a few more guidelines:

- Ensure that participants are under no pressure to give permission for the recording to be made.
- Do not participate in any recording made against a participant's wishes.

One form of pressure may be your own recruitment tactics! I am often very keen and (overly) enthusiastic when trying to recruit participants to be either audio or video-recorded. Just be aware of how you are trying to persuade people and, ideally, *seek their permission some time prior to the event.* You should also be aware of the possible pressures that can emerge when recording encounters between professionals and 'non-professionals', for example, counselling sessions or job interviews. At its most basic level, two courses of action can occur. The professional can just assume that the participant will be willing to be recorded, and, often indirectly, place undue pressure on the participant by talking for them: 'We have nothing to hide, do we?' Alternatively, the 'non-professional' may feel that to refuse could problematize that encounter and somehow transform that professional's actions towards them. Ideally, you should give the participants a way to contact you directly, so that after the event, if they change their minds, they can directly speak to you and ask for the recording to be destroyed. Also, in information sheets and whilst talking to them you should stress that refusing to take part (or acceptance) will not affect how they are treated.

A further guideline concerns knowing when to stop the recording:

- Stop the recording if the participant asks you to, or if it is having an adverse effect on the participant or research setting.

Obviously, if someone asks you to stop the recording, just turn the recording device off. However, knowing when something is having an 'adverse effect' can be quite a tricky one to judge, and again you need to stay aware. During a focus group I conducted, one of the participants was becoming very emotional and started using verbally abusive language. At one point I thought she could actually become physically violent towards others in the group. After I, and other participants in the group, tried to diffuse the situation, we quickly stopped the recording, so they she could relax and leave the space. I then went and had a very long conversation with her, dropped my researcher identity, and just listened to her story. Although this is a very extreme case, such 'emotionally charged' action is not unique. People can, and do, become incredibly involved in the situation. Research-led encounters (such as interviews and focus groups) can, at moments, become therapeutic or counselling environments or spaces where people offer very personal information. It is not your responsibility to become a 'counsellor' but it is your responsibility to be aware of the potential implications of your actions – especially when researching sensitive or emotive topics. It may be that you need to have access to the contact details of professional services or support groups.

We have three further points to consider:

- Do not use the recording for purposes outside the scope of the original consent for use, without obtaining further consent.
- Ensure that the recording does not compromise the participant's privacy and dignity.
- Make appropriate secure arrangements for storage of recordings.

One way we traditionally achieve these aims is through assuring all participants that all the information will be treated confidentially and that they will be made anonymous in any subsequent transcripts or research reports. *Confidentiality and anonymity* are usually achieved by:

- Never disclosing any personal identifying details of participants when talking to others, unless they are part of the project team.
- Removing all details that could identify either the specific participants or the precise location of the research site from any transcripts or research reports. Generally this refers to references to real names and places. You can encounter problems when your participants or the research sites are taken from a small community or practice. For example, when researching the social organization of a clinical practice guidelines development group (a multi-disciplinary group that evaluates the quality of research evidence on a specific medical condition and produces government-supported guidelines on best practice), one of my colleagues had to remove all references to the condition, research papers and specific treatments and drugs the group was reviewing. If any of these references had been included, anyone within that medical community would know exactly which group was being researched. Similarly, with the Women in Construction project, as there are so few women in very senior roles in the major companies in the construction industry, I had to remove references to the size and scope of the companies talked about by these participants. Video recordings or still images (including screen shots or screen grabs from videos) are often very difficult to anonymize in publications. Researchers often blank-out or smudge the faces of participants or produce line drawings of the images.

- Keeping all recordings and copies of any details that could identify participants (e.g. consent forms, recruitment records) in secured cabinets or drawers. Given today's technology, this includes keeping all the relevant electronic files or documents in secured files or on secure servers, where only you or the research team has access.
- Only playing the recordings to the research team. I should note that with some research projects, they specifically ask for consent to play the recordings in other spaces, for example, in academic meetings or workshops, at academic presentations or conferences, or in classrooms to students. More recently, given the concern to generate archives of qualitative data for other researchers to engage with, some ask for consent to reuse either transcripts and/or recordings for other research projects. Importantly, as you obtain written consent you should get them to consent to each type of usage of the recording.

When considering the dignity of participants you should also think about what information is actually fundamental for you to collect for the research project. For example, when video-recording some general practitioner/patient encounters, we positioned the camera so that it only focused on the desk in the consulting room and did not focus on the examination couch. As the project was concerned with how computers were used in the consultation, we felt that it was neither essential nor appropriate to film the patients on the examination couch. As such, we managed to maximize (part of) the patients' privacy and dignity as they very rarely had to appear in front of the camera whilst naked, semi-naked, dressing or undressing.

With some groups (notably children), a participant's privacy cannot always be guaranteed as certain legal issues can emerge. For example, a child in an interview could disclose the physical abuse they suffer from their parents, guardian or another child or illegal activities such as burglary or drug-taking. You should try to establish in advance whether full confidentiality will be provided if such topics are raised. Obviously, this will depend on the topic of the research. If the project is focused on children's experiences with illegal drugs and under-age drinking, you would provide them with full confidentiality agreements. Generally, if you are confronted with any such ethical dilemmas you should consult your supervisor, manager or related experts in the area.

Recordings in 'public spaces'

When making recordings in public spaces you generally have to follow different guidelines. How can you offer informed consent if you are video-recording people's conduct in a shopping mall, in a large hospital reception area or on a train platform? In such cases it would probably be impossible to seek consent from each person due to the sheer number of people who just wander into the view of the camera. You have to follow a different set of procedures. It is worth noting that none of those spaces is 'public' in one sense of the word: shopping malls are owned by companies, hospital reception areas and train platforms are always within an organization's jurisdiction, even public parks are maintained and owned by local councils. In such cases you generally need to seek permission from that specific organization prior to doing any filming. What is required of you will depend on the specific space you want to record in, the objectives of your recording and the demands of the specific organization. For example, von Lehm et al. (2001) were interested in how people conduct themselves in museums and galleries, especially how people look at, notice and interact with exhibits and other visitors. He had permission from the museum managers but was also required to place large signs near the cameras to inform members of the public that they were entering an area where recording was taking place. I also know that in the US you need to gain a specific consent from an ethics committee prior to conducting any recording in public spaces.

Some closing comments

Hopefully, these are all relatively clear points and how they relate to your research will depend on the specifics of your project. Thinking about the ethical implications of your research is never just a bureaucratic or organizational requirement or hurdle. It is essential to any research project. It is essential that anyone who wants to conduct research has *respect* for those people they are researching (and demonstrates this with their actions throughout the life of the project). If you want to take away one message, *be sensitive and aware of the possible implications of your actions*. Despite all the cautionary tales I have offered in this section, again I want to note that in the majority of situations, people are more than happy for you to record what they are talking about or what they are doing. Just remember to clearly inform them, to seek their consent. Above all, treat your participants with respect – they are never just 'mere data'.

Key points
- It is your duty to be aware of the relevant guidelines, recommendations or codes of ethical conduct that could apply to the research you undertake.
- Your research should not cause any harm or distress, either psychological or physical, to anyone taking part in it. Anyone taking part in the research should be aware that they are taking part in research, understand what the research is about and consent to take part in it.
- You should never place yourself in any potentially dangerous situations.

Further reading

These works treat ethical issues in more detail in general or for specific methods or approaches:

Barbour, R. (2007) *Doing Focus Groups* (Book 4 of *The SAGE Qualitative Research Kit*). London: Sage.

Economic and Social Research Council (2005) *ESRC Research Ethics Framework*. Online at http://www.esrc.ac.uk/ref; accessed on 21 Feb. 2006.

Flick, U. (2007a) *Designing Qualitative Research* (Book 1 of *The SAGE Qualitative Research Kit*). London: Sage.

Flick, U. (2007b) *Managing Quality in Qualitative Research* (Book 8 of *The SAGE Qualitative Research Kit*). London: Sage.

Kelly, M. and Ali, S. (2004) 'Ethics and social research', in C. Seale (ed.), *Researching Society and Culture* (2nd ed.). London: Sage, pp. 115–28.

Ryan, A. (2005) 'Ethical issues', in C. Seale, G. Gobo, J.F. Gubrium and D. Silverman (eds), *Qualitative Research Practice*. London: Sage, pp. 230–47.

4
The practicalities of recording

Chapter objectives
After reading this chapter, you should

- know more about certain very practical dilemmas, including what to record, how to record it, which parts of your recordings to transcribe and the level of detail of the transcripts;
- see that there are no definitive answers to any of these questions and that most depend on what your analytic approach is alongside the topic you are focusing on;
- know some fundamental points that may help you make certain decisions; and
- be aware that whatever you do, do not just rush into the field with, say, your video camera and note pad and assume that everything will go according to your well-developed plan.

Recording equipment

One piece of very vital equipment is the recording device. You generally need the following equipment:

- Audio recorder or video camera
- Audio- or videotapes (and some to spare)
- Additional batteries
- External microphone(s)

- Note pad and pen
- A good working knowledge of how to set up and use this equipment.

The last item on the list is very, very important. If you are not sure how to operate it, you will only worry throughout the encounter about whether or not it is working. Even when you know exactly how to operate the equipment, you can still make really 'stupid' mistakes. I have never (yet) failed to record at least part of a focus group or interview, but I have had the pause button down for part of an interview, had the equipment break, and managed to put the microphone in the wrong socket (and so had to transcribe a 'whispered' recording).

Currently, there is a great variety of audio recorders and video cameras. I am not going to outline specific models you could use, but I want to note some of the benefits and shortcomings of different types of recording devices.

Audiotape recorders

These are still the most commonly used devices. You should always try and connect *an external microphone* with this type of device. Some audiotape recorders do have an in-built microphone, but I never use these as they often pick up the noise of the 'engine' as well as the talk. Also, you have to be aware that you will often need to stop the recording and turn over the tape at some point during the encounter given the limited recording time of audiotapes. With most focus groups (and some in-depth interviews) you may have to change the tapes more than once. There are a number of easy-to-use transcribers currently available for audiotapes.

Minidisc recorders

These will generally produce a higher quality, clearer, recording than audiotape recorders. As very few of the devices have internal microphones, you will have to use an external microphone. They also allow for much longer recording time per disk, so you are unlikely to have to stop the encounter and change discs. They can be problematic when it comes to transcribing the recording, as there are currently no transcribers designed for minidiscs. This means you often have to either re-record the recording onto audiotape (to be able to use a transcriber) or have the technology and equipment available to download the recording onto a computer (to use a computer-based transcriber).

Digital or hard-disk audio recorders

These are devices that record the sound directly onto a computer chip within the device and produce a very high quality recording. They often have very good

35

quality internal microphones, so test the device to see whether an external microphone is necessary. Again, like mini-disk recorders, they offer a very long recording time, so you do not have to worry about missing any of the talk. They are designed to be directly connected to a computer so that the audio file(s) can be downloaded and stored very quickly and easily. The recording can then be played on a computer-based audio player. The only real shortcoming can be the cost of these devices compared to the other types given above. However, increasingly many of the MP3 players people typically use to play and download music on can also be used as recording devices.

Video cameras

You have the choice between

- *Analogue devices* – recording onto VHS or Hi8 tapes.
- *Digital devices* – recording onto Mini DV tapes, memory cards or DVDs.

Although some cameras have quite good microphones, it is generally necessary to use some form of external microphone as well. In some situations, you may want to use an additional wide-angled lens (which you thread onto the lens of your camera) and a tripod. To transcribe (and analyze) the recording, you can either use the appropriate video player or download the images onto the computer. If using a video player you often need to be able to produce a stable freeze frame (i.e. not fuzzy or jerky) and have good slow-motion facilities. Digital video cameras have recently become a lot more affordable and offer a better quality of recording and more stable image when viewing freeze frames or playing the tape in slow motion.

External microphones

These routinely come in two types, multi-directional and mono-directional. Mono-directional means, as the name suggests, that it picks up the sound from one general direction (often a 90° or 120° arc of sound), whereas multi-directional picks up 360° of sound. Mono-directional can work well in face-to-face interviews, but with focus groups and naturally occurring activities you should use multi-directional microphones. You can also get devices that consist of two multi-directional microphones, with long leads on both, that join together at a single microphone jack-plug. These are really useful for recording large focus groups or meetings on a single recording device, as they can be positioned at each end of the table or room.

The above review of possible recording devices is not at all extensive or detailed, but it offers you some things to consider. You often find that your choice of recording equipment is governed by what is currently to hand in the place where you study or work, what your budget is (if you have one) and what your friends and colleagues normally use or suggest you use. You should not worry that much, just play with the equipment before using it in a research setting and just be aware of the potential limitations of each device.

How do you know what to record?

You probably already have some ideas. You have read the relevant literature, you have some hunches and (maybe) have had a 'eureka' moment. And you realize that there is a gap in the literature or a topic that needs to be focused on from a slightly different angle.

Others have read your project outline – colleagues, funding agencies, supervisors, friends, ethical committees, representatives of your research site – and hopefully have offered you advice about what data to collect, and how and when to collect it. The courses of action you take next are dependent on your source(s) of recorded 'data'. Obviously, the practicalities of knowing what to record in a face-to-face interview are radically different from knowing what to record, say, in a video-based ethnography of how a legal office works.

I am now going to divide the following discussion into two areas. First, I am going to briefly focus on so-called 'researcher-initiated' recordings: interviews and focus groups (for a more detailed discussion see Kvale, 2007, and Barbour, 2007, in this series). I am then going on to focus on 'naturally occurring' interactions: audio- or video-based recordings and ethnography. As I noted in the previous chapter, the division between researcher-initiated and naturally occurring recordings is *very problematic* and so can be misleading, but for the moment, and to make both your and my own life easier, let us work with that binary. For each area, I am going to focus on three interrelated practices: recruitment, topical focus and the actual moments of recording.

The practicalities of interviews and focus groups

Recruiting participants

When generating interview and focus group data, *recruitment* is routinely the most challenging aspect. Be warned, it can be a very, very slow and 'tortuous' activity. Yet the process of finding participants and setting up interviews or focus groups is, as may be obvious, massively central to the outcomes of your research. Rubin and Rubin (1995) note four key areas around recruitment:

- finding knowledgable participants;
- getting a range of views;
- testing emerging themes with new participants; and
- choosing participants to extend results.

These are all very valuable ideals; however, the actual practice can deviate from this – like many things, recruitment routinely happens on an ad hoc and chance basis.

The actual problems of recruitment can vary dramatically. When accessing potential participants you have to follow many trails, often relying initially on chance meetings, friends and colleagues, and then on contacts given by other interviewees or focus group participants (this is often referred to as snowball sampling). It is important to *try* to get a range of views on the topic of your research, as those few participants who produce radically different or contrasting talk can often be central to modifying your theories. Above all, *it is vital to take some field notes about the recruitment process* and to offer it in reports of the research, as questions of access and recruitment can be central to understanding some of the outcomes of the research. For example, when trying to recruit general practitioners (GPs) to talk about how they deal with patients with alcohol problems, one GP told me, 'This is an important issue, but I'm not going to do an interview because I don't want to be known as the GP who is interested in alcohol problems in my practice'. His reluctance to take part and his concern that the GPs he works with might start sending patients with alcohol-related problems to him, documents a broader issue that the majority of GPs struggle with when dealing with their patients' alcohol problems. This discourse – constant struggle – was also a central theme in the subsequent interviews and focus groups.

Generating a list of questions and topics

So once you have arranged an interview or a focus group and sent out the relevant information sheets and consent forms, you have to consider what issues you want to cover with this specific interviewee or this specific focus group. Hopefully, you have already generated a general topic guide, outline or schedule. Whatever approach is taken, whether you produce a typed schedule on official headed paper or a handwritten list, it is useful to have something with you, be it 'key' words or written, 'finely crafted', questions. Also, in focus groups (and in some interviews) you may want to have some other resources pre-arranged, be they photographs, a video or a presentation to both focus and facilitate the group's discussions.

The actual content of the list of questions is *initially* generated in negotiation with the relevant academic and non-academic literature, alongside your thoughts and hunches about what areas *might* be important to cover in the interview. You need to be aware that *the questions you ask can change over the life-cycle of the project*. The list of questions I take to interviews or focus groups is always shifting in relation to various influences. They mutate in relation to the specific group or person I am with – my recruitment conversations on the phone with them, what I have read about them or been told about them. Also, this list is influenced by my conversations with my fellow researchers, what I have read in the recent literature, conferences I have attended, the interviews or focus group I have done previously or what is arising from the ongoing analysis.

I want to stress that you do not have to use *any* of the questions that you initially prepared. The point is to follow the participant's talk, to follow up on and *to work with them* and not strictly delimit the talk to your predetermined agenda. You do not have to ask the same question in the same way in each encounter. You often cover the same broad themes in different interviews or focus groups, either through the participants or you raising it as a subject for talk. This is a central rationale of interviews and focus groups – *that they enable you to gather contrasting and complementary talk on the same theme or issue*.

Recording

You have to make the decision on how you are going to record the research encounter. You generally have the following options:

- Note-taking after the encounter.
- Note-taking during the encounter.
- Audiotaping the encounter.
- Videotaping the encounter.

I always try to audiotape, for some very pragmatic reasons: *I want to interact with the participants,* I do not want to spend a lot of my time head down and writing. Also, the tape provides me with a much more *detailed record of the verbal interaction* than any amount of note-taking or reflection could offer. I can replay the tapes, produce transcripts, and then selectively draw on these to provide demonstrations of my argument.

Some people do record focus groups with video cameras (and some record face-to-face interviews with video cameras), but such video recording can raise some practical problems. The main question you need to ask is: *do you really need the additional information video data offer?* To be sure, video data offer you certain benefits:

- *A record of non-verbal conduct.* We all routinely use facial and bodily gestures and actions to elaborate the meaning of certain ideas or topics we are trying to convey.

- *An aid to the transcription process.* When you try to transcribe focus groups from audiotapes alone you are often very confused as to which person is saying a specific thing. It is often much easier to discover the identity of a speaker when you have the additional information offered by a video.

However, video recording has various potential costs:

- *Participants may be less likely to agree to take part.* Some participants feel that video recording is too intrusive and that an audio recording offers a higher degree of anonymity.
- *Participants may take a long time to get accustomed to the equipment.* It seems to take people less time to 'forget' about the presence of an audio recorder than a video recorder. Also, it is harder to ignore the presence of a video camera if it is constantly being operated by someone.
- *An additional researcher may have to operate the video camera.* It is not always easy to find a suitable place to position the camera so that all the participants (and the researcher) are caught within the camera's field of vision. This may be due to the shape of the room, where people are positioned or the size of the group. In such cases, you may just choose to position the camera to get the best possible shot, have multiple cameras, or ask someone to constantly operate the camera.

Whether the benefits outweigh the costs is intimately related to the research question you are undertaking. You should always ask, is the additional intrusion of a video camera, especially in respect to the intrusion of a participant's privacy, necessary?

No matter whether you record the encounter on audio- or videotape, you should also think about writing up your observations or impressions about the encounter. Typically, really interesting and relevant talk or action happens before or after the recording device is turned off. I always make notes as soon as is possible, often just after I or the participant(s) have left the research space. I usually record a description of what happened:

- in our initial stages prior to the recording device being switched on
- during the recording, and
- after the recording device had been switched off.

Whatever you do, make sure you do make some notes reasonably soon after the encounter as you will soon forget the salient points. I generally scribble down as many key points or phrases as I can remember and then write them up later that day or on the next day. The final description can range in detail from a paragraph covering each section (before, during and after recording) to much more extensive and elaborate descriptions. These descriptions can sometimes really enhance your understanding of that encounter. For example, when interviewing someone in a coffee shop we turned to the subject of his sexuality, and he began to speak in hushed tones. After the interview, when we left the café, he noted that 'This is a small community and I don't want to upset future business clients'. For this interviewee this was a problematic topic to talk about in such a public space and this enabled me to get a sense of why that topic was so abruptly changed. We then discussed this issue, the politics of sexuality and business, which helped me further refine my understanding of the topic.

The practicalities of audio- or video-based ethnographies

Recruiting participants

As with focus groups and interviews, recruitment is central to the trajectory of your research. However, you can have different considerations and (potential) problems to take into account. You will generally be seeking to record some kind of collective organizational activity *that would take place if you were not present*, say a team meeting or a one-to-one meeting between a professional and a client. You are very rarely just recruiting individual participants over a range of sites, but rather a *collection of participants within one research site* (or sometimes collections of people distributed over several research sites). I should note that much of what I say below about recruitment for audio- or video-based ethnographies is similar to when you undertake interview and focus group research with participants within a single organization. However, unlike interviews or focus groups, where you co-ordinate a specific group of people to speak with you and direct them to focus on your specific agenda, your aim is to record the encounters just as they routinely happen, without undue interference from you or your recording device(s).

Recruitment often occurs in three interrelated phases; you need to:

- contact someone in the research site who can facilitate initial access to that site;
- get permission from those who manage that specific research site; and
- get consent from the specific participants whom you will be recording.

I am going to offer two narratives from my own experiences (see Boxes 4.1 and 4.2) that outline how the above phases can occur in practice. One of them may appear quite scary, especially in the sense of how long the process can take, but remember it is only one example.

Box 4.1 Example 1: Medical decision-making in a hospital ward

I was having a conversation with one of my friends and she mentioned a study that she was about to start. She was going to interview medical professionals and patients in a specific unit of a hospital to understand how various treatment decisions were made. I noted that, rather than solely relying on what the patients and professionals tell her occurs, it could be really useful to have some recordings of the medical interactions as they happen.

Some weeks later my friend spoke to me and said that she had mentioned the idea to one of the lead clinicians who works in the unit and that the clinician was really interested. I was then invited to a meeting they were having about the interview study and briefly outlined my ideas for different ways of recording the decision-making process. The clinician was enthusiastic and said they would ask other members of their team what they felt about it. A month later, I was invited to visit the ward and was given a guided tour. I was introduced to all the members of the team (including administration staff, nurses and clinicians) and was asked to sit in on one consultation. The visit enabled them to ask me questions about the possible study and enabled me to gain a sense about what their work involved. I asked some questions about their specific procedures, routines, equipment and documentation. At the end of the visit I had an understanding about the feasibility of the study and realized, due to the mobile and distributed nature of their work, that it would be best to audio-record consultations and make field notes of the related work.

The next stage is to arrange funding and ethical approval, a process that can take anything from three months to a year, especially since research in medical settings has many layers of ethical approval. Prior to beginning the study I will visit the site several times and probably present the project at one of the unit's team meetings, where I can answer any of their questions. Prior to any period of observation or recording, I will then have to seek informed consent from all the medical professionals and any patients I observe.

Box 4.2 Example 2: Validating documents in team meetings

Again, with this project, I was initially approached by a friend. He was conducting an ethnography of an organization that publishes a lot of scientific information and reviews. He was asked by the manager of that organization to research how this information was produced. Part of the process involved a series of interdisciplinary team meetings to discuss, page by page, drafts of a specific document in order to amend and audit the quality of the information. He felt that video-recording the team meetings could be useful as a video would 'capture' both the discussion of the documents and could show at

(Continued)

(Continued)

exactly what moments the text of the document got referred to, quoted from and altered. He raised the idea of videoing the meetings with the co-ordinator of the specific group; she then raised it at their next meeting and he answered the team's questions. By the next meeting we had arranged permission and consent to begin recording the meetings. The whole process, from initially raising the possibility of recording the meetings to setting up video cameras in the meetings, took about two weeks.

As these examples demonstrate, *the actual time it takes to gain access to a site can vary dramatically*. In many research projects I conduct, I initially work with a specific individual when negotiating access to a research site. Such people are called *gatekeepers*, and they are often friends, friends of friends or colleagues, or, more rarely, emerge from chance encounters. On some occasions I have had to cold-call people to try to negotiate access, but this can make recruitment much more problematic. Once you have a contact, they can help co-ordinate your access to the site, and often act as a spokesperson for you in conversations with other members of the organization.

Generating a list of questions and topics

Unlike focus groups and interview-based research, with this type of research you are not explicitly directing the trajectory of participants' actions or talk. You set up the recording equipment and then let the action just 'happen'. However, to answer your research question(s) and follow up some of the topics you are interested in, you need to know what to record. It is obviously much easier to know what to record when the activities occur in and around one space and over set periods of time. Say, for example, you are interested in how debt counsellors advise clients. They probably have their own office or a specific meeting room where they advise clients, as well as arranging specific days and times when they see clients. But you may also discover that sometimes the rooms in which the sessions take place have to be changed at short notice and you have already spent time setting up the equipment in one room and did not bring a long enough extension lead to plug in the camera in the new room. Or you may discover that some of the work occurs over the phone and you did not bring an adapter to plug your audio recorder into the phone. Or maybe you discover that some of their advice work happens before and after clients leave, where they discuss cases with colleagues over coffee. Without a working knowledge of participants' work practices, you may not get the 'data' you need or want. The practical solution to avoid potential problems is *to conduct some ethnographic fieldwork prior to undertaking any audio or video recording*. The period of fieldwork can range from a very short visit to the research site, where you may shadow someone or just conduct an informal interview, to a series of extensive visits.

Conducting some kind of fieldwork not only enables you to get a sense of what 'data' you need and but also the limits of what you will be able to get through audio or video recording.

Through a period of fieldwork you can establish:

- What the participants' usual work routines are and talk to them about their work practices.
- Whether you need to see and understand the documents they use and whether it would be possible to get copies of any of these documents.
- Whether any of the activities, tasks or interactions are spatially or temporally distributed. Can you just set up your equipment in one room or do you need really portable equipment? Will certain days or times of day be better to visit than others?
- Whether they use any complex tools, equipment or technology that you will need to become familiar with. Will you need time to play with their equipment or need them to explain what they are doing and why?
- Whether they use any complex or specialized language, which you will need to become familiar with.
- What specific equipment you will need and where you will need to place it.

As the above list of ideas suggests, it is often essential to carry out some kind of fieldwork for a range of practical and methodological reasons. Such information will direct the trajectory of your research questions and topics, often refining your initial hunches as well as adding potential additional topics to focus on. As noted previously, it is quite normal for your focus to shift and mutate over the life-cycle of a project. After an initial round of working with your recordings (and field notes), you will probably return to the research site, either to collect additional recordings and/or to ask the participants questions about specific things that you observed on the recordings. You may also seek additional or alternative sites or situations to record, in order to understand how routine or typical the practices you have observed are.

Recording

You often enter a field site and have a hunch about what you need to record and how you would like to record it. You already know you going to make some form of written field notes. Irrespective of what sort of information would be ideal for your project, you have to ask two questions:

- What form of recording is acceptable to the participants?
- What form of recording is feasible in this specific site?

In some projects, with some participants, audio recording is the only acceptable form of recording. This can be connected to issues of confidentiality and/or levels of agreement to take part. As I noted above, some people can find the presence of a video camera too intrusive. Similarly, audio recording may be the only feasible or viable option, given the topics you are trying to understand. This is especially relevant when the participants are very mobile, say nurses in a hospital ward, where you would be trying to follow them, operate a camera and avoid obstacles (and avoid your movements obstructing others).

Audiotaping an encounter is generally a lot easier to co-ordinate. You only need to transport a small amount of equipment and it can be set up very quickly. Once you have positioned the microphone and tested the equipment – and please always remember to test it in your field site – it is relatively unobtrusive. Also, if you are unable to be present in the space while the encounter happens, most participants can operate it themselves, they can stop and start the recording and if necessary change the tapes for you. In some situations, like large meetings, you may need to use two audio recorders or alternatively use two multi-directional microphones that merge into a single microphone jack-plug.

Audiotaping can have disadvantages. For example Allistone's (2002) research focused on meetings between parents and school teachers. The meetings occurred in the teacher's classroom, with the child's parent(s) going into the classroom one at a time. By audiotaping these meetings he minimized the level of intrusion and also increased the numbers of parents who consented to have the meeting recorded. He sat outside the classroom, answered any of the parents' questions and confirmed that they had consented to take part. In between each session, he re-entered the room to change the tape. The disadvantage of this approach only became relevant once he was engaged in listening to and analyzing the tapes.

When listening to the tapes, Allistone noticed that prior to the initial announcement about the child's marks the teacher would often pause and then there would be what sounded like the 'shuffling' of paper. Once the shuffling had ceased, the teacher would deliver the news about that child's grades. It also sounded as though the teacher was reading from a document when they were delivering the news and sometimes teachers would preface the news by saying 'Well, Mr Brown's report says that ... '. Allistone realized that these reports, written by other teachers, were an essential resource to deliver 'bad' news about children's grades. By orientating the parents to the presence of a document, through searching for it and explicitly reading aloud from it (rather than just scanning it and summarizing the information), the teacher was trying to demonstrate to the parents that they were delivering *someone else's point of view*. This specific teacher was not the author of the bad news; rather, they were only reporting what another

45

teacher had said and so could not be held totally responsible by the parents. As he was relying solely on a verbal record of the encounter, Allistone could only presume the role of the documents, so he then spoke to one of the teachers in his study and she confirmed his hunch about document use. This story usefully demonstrates one of the potential disadvantages of relying only on audiotapes. If Allistone had been able to videotape the meeting or had been able to stay in the room whilst the recordings where being made (and taken some field notes), his attention may have been more rapidly focused on the role of document use. However, in saying that, document use was only one part of a whole range of resources teachers drew on when delivering bad news to parents.

Videotaping also has its advantages and disadvantages. You often need to transport a lot more equipment and it can take much longer to set up. Once you are at the research site, you have to make various decisions and often need to test out the camera in various places to get the best shot. It depends on what information you want. In most settings you will set the camera (or cameras) on a tripod, direct the camera at where the people are going to be working and then adjust the position and height of the tripod, the angle of the camera, and zoom in and out of the shot. Not every room offers you a great position to place the camera or a great field of vision to capture all the action and you may have to move furniture, use plug-extension leads or use more than one camera. Through prior fieldwork you should already be aware of what sort of actions you want to be able to record; they often include:

- the faces, gestures and (parts of) the bodies of participants;
- any tools or equipment or other objects they use; and
- any documents they use.

When it comes to filming computer screens, you should be aware that you will rarely see clearly what is occurring on the screen. For some technical reason, the image is generally very poor. If you need to constantly record the information on the screen, you will generally have to set up some kind of direct link between the computer and another video camera. *There is no perfect shot or angle,* you always have to work with the possibilities of the room and activities and realize that people will often shift about in chairs, move the chairs around or walk around the room. You also have to arrange a suitable place for the microphone and make sure that none of the wires could trip anyone up.

As a brief practical aside, you should be aware that microphone jack-plugs can cause stress on the microphone socket in the video camera. If you stretch the cable too far or it gets pulled (by someone tripping on the wire), the socket and/or jack-plug can become irreversibly damaged. So another piece of kit to have is some form of sticky tape – I always have duct tape and plumber's tape. I tape the microphone cable to the body of the video camera, or tripod, to allow some slack cable and reduce any pressure on the socket, and tape down any loose wires to the furniture or floor.

Finally, you have to consider whether you will be in the room when the activities take place, although you should realize that this is not always acceptable to the participants nor is it feasible to observe the encounter. You generally gain really useful information by observing, 'first-hand', what is going on rather than solely relying on an audio or video recording. You may be able to undertake a period of observational fieldwork (where you just sit in on some encounters), then on other occasions you could set up the equipment and leave the setting. Obviously, if you are going to be constantly operating the video camera, so that you can direct the camera onto an ever-moving and shifting scene, you will be in the space by default. However, in saying that, it is often best just to set up the equipment on a tripod, work out the best angle and then leave it alone. When you constantly operate or 'fiddle with' equipment, your actions can soon become the centre of attention and so unduly influence the encounter. No matter what you do, the presence of the recording equipment and/or your own physical presence will influence the scene *to some extent*. The point is to reduce the extent of your 'contribution' to the encounter and be sensitive to the possible effect you have had.

Some closing comments

If the above descriptions of the practicalities of recording make all this sound like a lot of work or make it all sound very difficult or complicated, I must apologize. Trust me it is not. It is just that I have tried to offer you a detailed account of these very routine courses of actions that you often have to go through. Whenever you offer that level of detail (and I could have gone into a lot more), you can produce what you would have just taken for granted, and just got on with, as quite technical and challenging. So try and read my above descriptions as aide-mémoires or things to consider (however briefly) rather than understand them as things 'I have to do' or problems 'I will face'.

Key points
- Learn about your recording equipment prior to entering the field. Just keep playing with it as often as you can.
- Realize that gaining access to the field (and working in the field) will often take up much more of your time than you initially imagined.
- Stay flexible. Be prepared to modify your ideas about what constitutes the best sources and opportunities to record 'data'.

Further reading

The following works give you some more advice about how to record your data:

Barbour, R. (2007) *Doing Focus Groups* (Book 4 of *The SAGE Qualitative Research Kit*). London: Sage.

Branley, D. (2004) 'Making and managing audio recordings', in C. Seale (ed.), *Researching Society and Culture* (2nd edn). London: Sage, pp. 207–24.

Goodwin, C. (1994) 'Recording human interaction in natural settings', *Pragmatics* 3(2): 181–209.

Kvale, S. (2007) *Doing Interviews* (Book 2 of *The SAGE Qualitative Research Kit*). London: Sage.

ten Have, P. (1999) *Doing Conversation Analysis: A Practical Guide*. London: Sage, chap 4.

5
Transcribing audio and video materials

Chapter objectives
After reading this chapter, you should

- see the different ways that you can transcribe the recordings that you generate; and
- know from some materials that I have collected – a recording of people preparing a meal – some of the different levels of detail that you can add to transcripts of the same recording.

Harvey Sacks (1984), one of the pioneers of conversation analysis, outlines the rationale behind using recording equipment:

I started to work with tape-recorded conversations. Such materials had a single virtue, that I could replay them. I could transcribe them some-what and study them extendedly – however long that might take. The tape-recorded materials offered a 'good enough' record of what happened. Other things, to be sure, happened, but at least what happened on tape had happened.... I started with tape-recorded conversations ... simply because I could get my hands on it and I could study it again and again, and also, consequentially, because others could look at what I had studied and make use of it what they could, for example if they wanted to be able to disagree with me. (1984, p. 26)

Audio, and increasingly video, recordings of talk and interactions, although *never a comprehensive record of what is going on*, allow us access to many of the practices of social life.

As Sacks notes, people can only transcribe recordings 'somewhat'; transcripts are by their very nature *translations* – they are always partial and selective textual representations. The actual process of making detailed transcripts enables you to become familiar with what you are observing. You have to listen/watch the recording again and again (and again …). Through this process you begin to notice the interesting and often subtle ways that people interact. These are the taken-for-granted features of people's talk and interaction that without recordings you would routinely fail to notice, fail to remember, or be unable to record in sufficient detail by taking hand-written notes as it happened. What is key to remember is that *you base your analysis on the recording and your field notes.* Transcripts (and recordings) are only, to borrow Spiegelberg's phrase, 'aids for the sluggish imagination' (cited in Garfinkel, 1967, p. 39); they can help you remember 'what was going on' at the site you were observing. The subsequent benefit of making transcripts is that you can use them in the presentations of your findings.

To allow you some access to the range of processes involved, I am going to use some materials that I actually collected: a video recording of some people preparing a meal together.

Introducing the recording

I made this recording myself specifically with this book in mind. I needed something through which I could show both how to transcribe actual talk as well as 'non-verbal' features, such as hand gestures and how people manipulate objects. This meant I had to work with video recordings. I also wanted to provide still images from these recordings so that you could begin to see what I was talking about. Purely written descriptions of non-verbal activities are notoriously hard to follow and still images of them can really help demonstrate the point that you are making. However, as I wanted to use still images I would either have to get the participants' permission and the appropriate ethics committee approval – if the recording was from one of my field sites – or seek permission from the holder of the copyright on the images – if the recording was from a television programme. The obvious solution was to generate a new recording and specifically ask the participants' permission to use it in this book.

The easiest and quickest route was to ask if I could record some of my friends 'doing something'. I needed this thing to be a relatively spatially bounded activity, as I did not want to follow them round with a camera all day, or have to stand behind the camera and constantly change the angle of the shot. I needed something for which I did not have to seek an ethics committee approval or other organizational approvals, so all medical contexts and all work contexts were excluded. I also needed something that was not too technical or specialized, that would be hard to follow without actually having some inside knowledge of the work or organizational routines. Centrally, I wanted something that involved people in a shared task, as I wanted some talking to go on. In the end I asked some friends whether I could record them doing something 'at home'. So we agreed that I would record them (and me) collectively working to prepare a meal. And obviously, this had the added bonus that I would get to eat and drink with them as well.

The above list and related understanding of what some people might call 'selection criteria' is important. A camera lens co-ordinates the field of vision of a particular photograph or video recording and so produces a specific way of seeing and knowing that scene. Similarly, such factors as the needs and demands of ethics committees and organizations, research projects' outputs and technologies' capacities shape and limit the specific ways that any research can see, know and describe the world. Importantly, *recordings and transcripts themselves are always selective and always partial.* You can never offer a 'complete' transcript of a scene; as you will see below, even in a couple of minutes of interaction, far too much goes on to offer anything like a comprehensive level of detail.

Describing the scene

At the simplest level, a transcript can merely be *a description of the recorded event.* Providing a description is the most common way we seek to render actions and interaction available to others, both in our capacity as researchers and in our more routine everyday position of giving an account about something we witnessed. You might expect a transcript to have specific form or style or maybe to attend to some specific rules. As you transform some audio or video material, or your actual experience of that ongoing scene, into a written or verbal description, you are engaging in a version of transcription.

One way to describe the scene that is the focus for this section is to say this:

Ben has been asked to prepare a cucumber – to peel and de-seed it. Mary and Tim offer Ben two different, contrasting, ways to prepare that cucumber.

51

Now that does describe the scene quite well, although it gives you, the reader, very little access to how that specific interaction emerged and transformed. After I have watched the video, I could add more detail, and say this:

Ben has been asked to prepare a cucumber – to peel and de-seed it. Prior to preparing the cucumber, Mary notices that the cucumber is frozen. She leans over the table, picks up the cucumber in one hand, picks up a knife in the other and then starts to inspect it, turning it over in her hands. She smiles and she waits for a gap in the talk between Ben and Tim and then says, with some humour in her voice, 'It's frozen' ...

Now that offers a further level of detail and I could go on to describe the whole scene in this way – and just one minute of interaction could take up about the next five pages. Obviously, I could offer you a more detailed narrative – which would take up most of this book – or a less detailed account, say one page. And much of the time you work with recordings you often provide this sort of narrative description. Sometimes that is all you provide, sometimes you give an account just prior to the text of a transcript, to inform the reader about what has gone on in the encounter just prior to the moment described in the transcript. And this kind of work always occurs as you analyze your transcript – as you work to 'flesh out' or 'give life' to the transcript.

Through providing some version of a transcript you are always trying to give readers *access* to what you were able to witness (either first-hand and/or via recordings). The question you will always face is, what level of detail do I provide? One option is to only provide a narrative account, the other is to provide some form of more *structured description*, and it is how to create and use these more structured descriptions that the rest of this chapter will explore.

A basic transcript

The most common option is to offer some form of *verbatim transcript*, where you try to document the words that were spoken alongside who spoke them. In making the transcript (Extract 1 below) I have listened to this same sequence between seven and ten times (but bear in mind I was being very, very fussy about the quality). As I was working from a digital video recording, I had already downloaded the recording on to my computer and just used an easily available (and free) media player. Initially I just played the sound without watching the image. When working with audiotapes or digital sound files downloaded onto your computer it is really useful to be able to use some form of transcriber or computer package that is foot-pedal operated. With audiotapes you should try to use a transcriber – a machine that when you stop the tape automatically rewinds a set amount of the tape. This means that when you press play again, you can re-listen to the talk just prior to when you stopped the tape, and so do not miss any of the words or have to constantly rewind it. The foot-pedal makes this whole process even easier as you can operate all the functions – stop, play, rewind and fast-forward – with your foot. You can now get computer packages that fulfil a similar purpose and that also come with a foot-pedal. Using a transcriber will save you masses of time and frustration. With practice and with the use of some form of transcriber, a very basic verbatim transcript of a two-party interaction (say a one-to-one interview) should take about *six to eight hours for one hour of tape*.

With the sound file of Extract 1 below, the first time I just listened to the talk and tried to make sense of the scene. I then opened up a blank document on my computer, replayed the file, and attempted to type all that I could hear. I paused the recording every now and again so that my typing could catch up with what I was hearing. I then replayed the whole sound file again and checked my first draft of the talk, again pausing the recording to amend the transcript. I kept repeating this process and kept amending parts of the transcript – be it changing whole words, changing who the speaker was or adding additional words – until I was reasonably happy with what I had done.

The setting for Extract 1 is a large kitchen where three people, Ben, Mary and Tim, are cooking a meal. The camera has been positioned on a tripod, against one wall of kitchen. At the point we enter the scene Mary and Ben are sitting opposite each other at a large table. Mary has just put down a glass of wine, leaned over the table towards Ben and picked up a cucumber. Tim is standing next to the hob, chopping vegetables on the work surface and frying something in a frying pan. We enter the action as Mary notes that the cucumber is frozen.

Extract 1 (The politics of cucumbers: Kitchen10: 2.17–3.17)

1	**Mary**:	It's frozen.
2		(Pause)
3	**Tim**:	Is it?
4	**Mary**:	Yeah ((laughs)). I don't think you can use it
5		(Pause)
6	**Ben**:	It is frozen
7	**Mary**:	Yeah. The bottom of the fridge is
8	**Ben**:	Ice cold
9	**Mary**:	Yeah. I'll see if there's part of it that isn't
10		(Pause)
11	**Mary**:	Yeah.
12	**Tim**:	Is it all frozen?
13	**Mary**:	No, this part of it's fine. Okay, when you peel it
14	**Ben**:	Uh huh
15	**Mary**:	slice it in four lengthways
16	**Ben**:	Oh and then just ((overlap))
17	**Mary**:	a n d t h e n ((overlap)) just take the seeds out

18	**Tim:**	Or alternatively slice it in half and use a teaspoon
19		and run it along
20	**Mary:**	You can choose whichever method you prefer
21	**Tim:**	And obviously there is going to be politics ((Mary
22		laughs)) depending on which method you choose
23	**Mary:**	Absolutely. No there won't.
24	**Ben:**	Secretly there will be though
25	**Mary:**	Heh?
26	**Ben:**	Secretly there will be ((Mary laughs))

I had to decide just how to represent the dynamics of the recorded talk – to make various choices about what I should put in, how I should put it in and what I should leave out. I want to briefly outline some of the decisions I made in producing this transcript, to give you access to some things you may to want to consider when producing your own transcripts.

First, notice the title of the transcript – I have called this 'Extract 1'. Researchers often use various words to mark specific sections of their reports as transcripts. The most common is calling these texts 'extracts'; others use the term 'transcripts' and others prefer 'fragments'. There is a politics to these descriptors. For example. the term 'fragment' denotes that what is shown is only a fragment, only a piece or slice of the ongoing scene, it is in no way documenting all of the actions and interactions of the ongoing scene. This sense of the partiality of transcripts connects into my urge to understand all my transcripts as *demonstrations*. I like the sense of demonstration as it connects to the multiple work that transcripts do: they demonstrate for the reader what was going on at that specific point in the interaction as well as demonstrate for the reader that particular part of my analytic argument.

Second, notice the text in parentheses, which makes part of the title. I have given this extract of this sequence of the talk both a more descriptive title – 'The politics of cucumbers' – and a more technical title – 'Kitchen10: 2.17–3.17'. What I have called the *technical title* is quite an important feature, as this code enables me to very quickly identify just where this extract comes from. In this case, I know it is from the original videotape that I have given the name 'Kitchen' and that it is the tenth clip that I downloaded onto my computer (which I gave the file name 'Kitchen Clip 10'). If I look in that file and fast-forward it to approximately two minutes seventeen seconds into the video (hence 2.17) and then play it until approximately three minutes seventeen seconds, I will be able to listen (and watch) the original recording. The more *descriptive title* – 'The politics of cucumbers' – is there so that I can, at a glance, just know which stretch of talk this is. In that sense it works as a mnemonic, it is an aid to my memory. This is more important with longer stretches of talk, where you might not want to have to read all the transcript to remember just why, all those months ago, you transcribed it or marked it as important.

The point is not to use my specific system of coding but rather to *develop some way to mark extracts in such a way so that you can easily find where they came from* – which section of the transcript or recording you have taken them from – and then be able to re-listen to the tape and/or re-read the broader section of the transcript to re-check your hunches or ideas.

Third, notice that each speaker is identified on the left-hand side of the transcript. In this extract we have three speakers: Tim, Mary, and Ben. What difference would it make to how you read the extract if I called them say 'A, B and C' or 'Man1, Woman, Man2' or 'Friend, Mother and Son'? However you label the speakers, you can offer a specific reading of the interaction. This is especially clear when transcribing more formal interactions, say teacher/pupil or salesperson/ customer encounters. In such cases you may well decide to use more formal categories like 'doctor' and 'patient' over the less formal version of using first names (which we can generally read gender from) over more neutral titles like 'A' or 'B'. You just need to think about what categories are relevant to use; a good rule of thumb is often to *use the descriptors that are relevant to and available to those taking part in the encounters.* For example, when transcribing many primary care consultations, 'doctor' and 'patient' (or the abbreviations of 'GP' or 'Dr' and 'Pt') may be most relevant, given that those people in the interaction will often be orientating to these identities and the work of being a patient and being a general practitioner. However, you should not to allow those more formalized categories to override your analysis because, at some points, they may well be doing friendship.

It is worth noting that with transcripts you often only see the people who are actually talking; others may not have spoken but may be present, say a researcher or a co-worker. These silent witnesses are not always visible in transcripts, especially ones based on audio recordings, but may be relevant to the trajectory of the talk at that point.

Fourth, note that each line has been given a number. When writing about an extract this enables you to quickly refer to a specific section of the talk without having to reproduce that section in the text. You have various options when it comes to line numbers. Sometimes you may only want to mark every fifth line, so only lines 1, 5, 10, 15, etc., would have the corresponding numbers of 1, 5, 10, 15, etc. This can be useful when you reproduce very long sections of talk and are not referring in any great detail to what occurs on specific lines. At other times you may only want to give each person's turn of talk a specific line number. And a turn can be a single word to a whole paragraph. Again, this can be useful when you only want to refer in broad detail to what is going in the talk. The option is yours about how you produce line numbers and you will probably develop a personal preference as to which style you use. Some word-processing packages offer the option to automatically put in line numbers as you type. This can be useful, especially when transcribing interviews or very long stretches of talk.

Finally, note how I have rendered the participants' talk, how I have given it a textual form. Each speaker appears to speak in lines and this gives the sense that they are all taking reasonably specific turns at talking. However, as we are all aware, talk is not always this ordered and, with this transcript, I have attempted to render just a few of the nuances of talk. For example, with lines 16, through marking 'Oh and then just' (16) with the words '((overlap))' I have tried to show where the speakers overlap their talk. By overlap I mean that as Ben says the words 'Oh and then just' Mary also says the words 'and then' (17) at the same time. As we will see below, when we come to see Jeffersonian-style transcript, there are other, more technical ways to render this interactional work.

Also, instead of writing the word 'just', I could have written it as '*jus*' as the 't' sound of the word is missing from Ben's talk. And I could have produced a more phonetic transcript as many of the words are not produced as grammatically coherent as they appear in Extract 1. For example, in line 21, I have written 'going to be', but it may have been more accurate – although less grammatical – to write 'gonna be'. With one of the Ben's utterances, 'Uh huh', on line 14, I have just tried to textually reproduce his response token. Such sounds or utterances like 'Uh huh' or 'heh?' are sometimes referred to as paralinguistic features of talk. As you can see, you have the choice between following the speakers' versions of word production and a more grammatical, textual style.

In Extract 1, I have also added other interactional features like laughter (4, 21, 26), a questioning tone (3, 12, 25) and pauses (2, 5, 10). An obvious question to ask is, how long are these periods of verbal silence that I have called a pause? I could have given the time of these pauses in seconds: the pause at 2 is approximately 3 seconds long, the pause at 5 is approximately 6 seconds long and the pause at line 10 is approximately 4 seconds long. What would such a description have added to this specific transcript? Also, should I have added the other moments where pauses of about one second occur – say in line 4, in between Mary laughing and saying 'I don't'? In asking these questions, I am aware that there is no wrong or right answer. You have a multitude of options as to what to include and what to exclude and how to render what you decide to include.

A question of detail

You have to make choices and choice is often between some degree of 'tight' or 'loose' coherence with the recording which you are working from. The tighter the coherence, the more technical your transcript will have to become. By technical I mean that you will have to use a specific series of notation devices to transmit the various interactional features you are trying to represent – and you will have to give other readers access to the notation that you decide to use. Poland (2002), albeit referring to interview transcripts, has developed a really useful list of things that he feels should be included in transcripts (see Box 5.1).

Box 5.1   Poland's instructions for transcribers

It is important for qualitative research that transcripts be verbatim accounts of what transpired in the interview (or any other context), that is, they should not be edited or otherwise 'tidied up' to make them 'sound better'.

Pauses	Denote short pauses during talking by a series of dots (…), the length of which depends on the amount of time elapsed (e.g. two dots for less than half a second, three dots for one second, four dots for one and half seconds). Denote longer pauses with the word pause in parentheses. Use '(pause)' for two- to three-second breaks and '(long pause)' to indicate pauses of four or more seconds.
Laughing, coughing, etc.	Indicate in parentheses; for example '(coughs)', '(sigh)', '(sneeze)'. Use '(laughing)' to denote one person, '(laughter)' to denote several laughing.
Interruptions	Indicate when someone's speech is broken off mid-sentence by including a hyphen (-) at the point where the interruption occurs (e.g. 'What do you-')
Overlapping specch	Use a hyphen to indicate when one speaker interjects into the speech of another, include the speech with '(overlapping)' then return to where the original speaker was interrupted (if he or she continues). For example: R: He said that she was impos- I: (overlapping) Who, Bob? R: No, Larry.
Garbled speech	Flag words that are not clear with square brackets and question mark, if guessing what was said (e.g. 'At that, Harry (doubled? glossed?) over'). Use x's to denote passages that cannot be deciphered at all (number of x's should denote approximate number of words that cannot be deciphered). For example, 'Gine went xxxxxx xxxxx xxxxx, and then (came? went?) home'.

(Continued)

(Continued)

Emphasis	Use caps to denote strong emphasis, for example 'He did WHAT?'
Held sounds	Repeat the sounds that are held, separated by hyphens. If they are emphasized, capitalise them as well. For example 'No-o-o-o, not exactly' or 'I was VER-r-r-y-y-y happy'.
Paraphrasing other	When a speaker assumes a voice that indicates he or she is parodying what someone else said or is expressing an inner voice in their head, use quotation marks and/or indicate with '(mimicking voice)'. For example: R: Then you know what he came out with? He said (mimicking voice) 'I'll be damned if I'm going to let YOU push ME around'. And I thought to myself: 'I'll show you'.

From: Poland (2002, p. 641).

The question of what level of notation to use is intimately tied to how you are engaging with your data. The level of detail I offered with Extract 1 above was chosen to demonstrate a relatively basic level of transcription. In saying that, this is far from the simplest level of transcription. When you read articles reporting quotes from interviews, you often lose the interactional nature of those encounters as things like interviewers' questions, pauses, response tokens (words like uh huh, yeah, and so on), tone and laughter are rarely given.

In reading Extract 1 above, I hope you got some sense of the encounter, some sense of the verbal, interactional, work of the speakers. That extract only covers one minute of the encounter and it took quite some time, roughly ten minutes, to transcribe to the level of detail that I was happy with. After that time I was pretty sure that I had got the words correct, got the word order correct and given you a sense of the other interactional features. In saying that, as I re-listened to the recording, whilst I was writing the above section to accompany the transcript, I still had to add a couple of words and add one of the pauses. This shows two important things:

- Try not to undertake all of your analysis from just the transcripts of a recording.
- Transcripts are living, evolving, documents – they are always susceptible to change and alterations.

I personally do not like doing *any* analysis from just transcripts alone. I find them rather flat reproductions of interactions as you can easily be 'misled' about just what is it that is going on and miss the nuances that you gain from hearing a specific tone or voice or pace of speech. In one data session I was involved in, I remember the group discussing a transcript at some length, prior to listening to the tape. Our understanding that a section from an interview was quite strained and slow-paced was transformed once we heard the tape: what appeared on the page as overly cautious questioning by the interviewer was re-heard as quite direct.

Through re-listening to your recordings you constantly re-engage with just what it is that is going on at specific moments in that encounter. Equally, as your analytic direction changes, so too might your need for a more nuanced and textured transcript. I now want to turn to a specific style or genre of transcription, most often used by those undertaking some form of conversation analysis or discursive psychology. For people undertaking this form of analysis it is vital to understand and document a very fine level of interactional detail.

A Jeffersonian transcript

In the 1960s, Gale Jefferson developed a specific style of transcription notation that was designed to use symbols found on a typewriter in order to render certain aspects of talk that are found in everyday interactions. This notation system is now very widely used and has almost become an industry standard, or baseline, for those undertaking forms of conversation analysis. Box 5.2 outlines the main features that are used by the people undertaking this style of work.

Box 5.2 Simplified Jeffersonian transcribing conventions

Symbol	Example	Explanation
(0.6)	that (0.5) is odd?	**Length of silence** measured in tenths of a second.
(.)	right (.) okay	**Micro-pause**, less than two-tenths of a second.
:::	I:::: I don't know	Colons indicate **sound-stretching** of the immediately prior sound. The number of rows indicates the length of prolonged sound.

(Continued)

(Continued)

_____	I <u>know</u> that	Underlining indicates **speaker's emphasis or stress**.
(	T: (Well at's R: (I mean really	Left brackets indicate the point at which one speaker **overlaps** another's talk.
=	you know=I fine	Equal sign indicates that there is **no hearable gap** between the words.
WORD	about a MILLION	Capitals, except at beginnings, indicate a marked **rise in volume** compared to the surrounding talk.
°	°Uh huh°	Words in degree signs indicate **quieter** than the surrounding talk.
> <	>I don't think<	Words in 'greater than' then 'less than' signs are delivered at a **faster pace** than the surrounding talk.
< >	<I don't think>	Words in 'less than' then 'greater than' signs are delivered at a **slower pace** than the surrounding talk.
?	Oh really?	Question mark indicates **rising intonation**.
.	Yeah.	Full stop indicates **falling intonation**.
Hhh	I know how .hhh you	A row of h's prefixed by a dot indicates an **inbreath**, without dot, an outbreath. The number of h's indicates the length of the in- or outbreath.
( )	What a ( ) thing	Empty parentheses indicate **inability to hear** what was said.
(word)	What are you (doing)	Word in parentheses indicates the **best possible hearing**.
(( ))	I don't know ((coughs))	Words in double parentheses contain **author's descriptions**.

Adapted from Jefferson (2004).

This can appear as an overly technical and complex way of textually reproducing talk. When you first encounter transcripts written using this notation system it is often hard to make sense of the text and imagine just what the talk sounded like. When I first attempted to read Jeffersonian-style transcripts, I routinely had to have a photocopy of the symbols in front of me to enable and guide my reading. I also used to say the lines out loud, trying to understand just how the symbols modify the sound and pace of words. It takes a bit of practice, but they do become more and more readable and intelligible after a short period of time. It also makes more sense when you can listen to a recording of the talk alongside a transcript.

I have re-transcribed *part* of Extract 1 below, this time adding more detail to the transcript by using some of the Jeffersonian symbols.

Extract 1.1 (re-transcribed section of Extract 1)

1	**Tim**:	Is it all frozen?=
2	**Mary**:	=No. this part of it's fine. Okay, when you pee::l it,
3	**Ben**:	°Uh huh°
4	**Mary**:	sli:ce it in fou:r.=lengthways (a n d t h e n)
5	**Ben**:	(Oh and then jus)
6	**Mary**:	just take the seeds out=
7	**Tim**:	=Or alternatively slice it in ha::lf, and use a <u>t</u>easpoon,
8		((banging sound)) and run it along.
9		(0.3)
10	**Mary**:	You can <u>ch</u>oose whichever method you, pre:<u>fer</u>.=
11	**Tim**:	=(And) obviously there is gonna be politics. (.)
12		(depending on which method you choose)=
13	**Mary**:	(>h u h< h e h h e h h e: h) =<u>Absolutely</u>.
14		((rustling sound))
15		(0.4)
16	**Mary**:	No there won't.=
17		=((banging sound))
18		(0.8)
19		((rustling sound))=
20	**Ben**:	=Secretly there will be though
21		(0.4)
22	**Mary**:	Heh?
23	**Ben**:	SECRETLY THERE WILL BE=
24		=ehh °heh heh heh°

First, go back to Extract 1 above and flip between the two transcripts and notice the differences between them. As you can see I have taken lines 12–26 of Extract 1 and re-transcribed them. What was fifteen lines long in Extract 1 is now twenty-four lines in total. So the actual level of detail and amount of symbols have massively increased. Now re-read Extract 1 and then read Extract 1.1 and try to compare each line. Obviously Extract 1 is easier to read, as it uses quite standard orthography, whereas Extract 1.1 will probably be quite tough going and you will need to refer to Box 5.2 to make some sense of the talk.

So have you gained anything – other than maybe saying to yourself 'why bother?' and an initial feeling of frustration? For me, the gain is a more textured re-description of the scene. You now have a sense of the quite artful and beautiful ways that we all routinely interact. The transcript begins to re-describe the masses of fine-grained interactional work that these speakers are engaging in while just getting on with having a chat and collectively cooking. For example, look at all the moments in the transcript where I've used the '=' sign. The equals sign is used to denote where there is no hearable gap between the words, where either:

- *One speaker latches one word to the next.* For example, in line 4 where Mary says 'sli:ce it in fou:r.=lengthways', the words 'four' and 'lengthways' almost bleed into each other. She stretches the end of the word 'four' so that it sounds something like 'fouuur' and has a slightly falling intonation and a slight decrease in volume as if maybe she is marking the end of that part or phase of her instruction on how to prepare this cucumber. As she produces the word 'lengthways', she speeds up the pace of her talk and it sounds as though the two words flow into one another. So she works to tag this additional important feature to just that specific phase of her instruction on how to prepare this cucumber through latching her talk.
- *One speaker latches their talk to a prior speaker's talk.* For example, in line 7 Tim says '=Or alternatively slice it in ha::lf,' and begins to offer an alternative instruction on how to prepare this cucumber. Mary in line 6 has given the last part of her instruction, Tim has obviously heard this as the last part of her instruction and at just the point that she stops speaking, Tim immediately starts his talk. In this way, his alternative set of instructions are latched onto the prior instructions and there is no hearable gap in the flow of talk or the flow of potential ways to prepare this cucumber.
- *One speaker latches their talk to a prior sound.* For example, in line 19 I have given a description of a sound that that I can hear that can only be described as a 'rustling sound' (on the video the sound is produced by Mary as she puts a bag of food on a work surface). As that sound ends, Ben starts to talk. In this way Ben demonstrates how we also produce our talk in time not only with others and our own talk but to various sounds in the ongoing scene.

Now that is just one example of how such a detailed transcript can demonstrate some of the features of a recording. Importantly, as noted earlier, both you and others who want to understand your work – but do not have access to the original recording – can gain some access to these fine-grained features.

I also want to note a few other differences between the two versions of the transcript. For example, in Extract 1, I simply noted some things in double parentheses like people speaking in overlap and people laughing and left some other things out, like the banging and rustling sounds. In Extract 1.1, I have marked where the speakers overlap, through square brackets, and attempted to transcribe the moments of laughter. Also, note how with some words I have underlined either whole words or part of those words to try and demonstrate how the speakers add some form of vocal stress to them. A word of caution on transcribing long sequences of laughter, crying or similar sounds: it is very likely to drive you crazy and utterly infuriate you. You can spend a huge amount of time trying to textually capture just what the sound is like and then you end up changing it as you re-listen.

When producing such detailed transcripts you need to realize that it takes both a lot of practice and a lot of your time. It took me about 30 minutes to re-transcribe the whole of that extract – and I am reasonably out of practice. I have been told that *it takes about eight hours to transcribe 15 minutes of talk to a Jeffersonian level of detail*. I am not sure how accurate that is because I have never timed myself and I have certainly never just transcribed for a whole day.

When transcribing Extract 1.1, I spent a lot of time just playing back very short sections of it trying to pick specific features out. When you start transcribing to this level of detail *it can be really helpful to work with someone else*, to jointly work on the same recording and help each other out both with what you heard and how to reproduce it on the page. It can also help to just focus on one thing at a time, for example pauses, stress or overlapping. You have various options when timing pauses. The low-tech way is to use the words 'one-one-thou-sand, two-one-thou-sand, three-one-thou-sand' and so on. Each section lasts about one second and each part represents about 0.2 of a second. Start saying this as soon as someone stops speaking and note when the speaker overlaps with the word. So, for example, if you manage to say 'one-one' and then the speaker comes in, then the pause is about 0.4 seconds. Replay that part of the recording and try it again to check your hearing. Another option is to use a stop-watch and a more technical solution is to play your recording through a computer package that enables you to time pauses. For me, the utterly precise timing of a pause is less important than the presence of a pause, and how, if at all, people respond to that pause.

Working versus reporting transcripts

Deciding what level of detail to transcribe something to is an important decision. You really have to think about transcribing in two stages. The first stage is the generation of your *working transcript*. This is the document that you work with on a day-to-day basis. You develop it through repeated listening (and/or watching) of your recordings. It gets changed, altered and modified along the way and often covered with analytic comments. It is only a device to help you remember what is going on in that specific recording, a way to guide your understanding. In one way it is a device that enables you to *slow down* what you are listening to (and/or seeing), to be able to capture and reflect on some of the features of the scene. It can *never* be a complete record of that encounter. The level of detail is dependent on what you are exploring; if you are fascinated by how interaction happens on a moment-by-moment level, you may well end up working with something close to a Jeffersonian transcript.

Your working transcript will probably have a higher level of detail than any you produce in reports. It is better to over-transcribe something – to add the features as you notice them, rather than restrict your attention to only transcribing what you initially feel is needed. Even if you are not doing conversation analytic-style work, if you notice particular stress on certain words, a particular rhythm of speech or laughter, or a particular sequence of overlapping talk in an argument, that may well help you understand just what it is that is going on. In saying all this, I cannot stress enough that your primary way to understand what is going on is to constantly re-engage with your recordings; *the transcript is always secondary, a memory device*.

The second stage of transcribing is your *reporting transcript* – the document that will be in your final report or thesis and (hopefully) publications. You need to be able to provide your readers with enough detail – enough textual evidence – for them to see just why you made that specific analytic point in relation to the transcript. As such, including *all* the detail you have noted down may be unnecessary to extending just that piece of your argument.

Working with video-based data

The transcripts given above have only offered you access to the verbal interactional work. And as I noted at the start, I actually videoed this encounter so I also have a mass of other interactional work that enhanced the participants' (and my analytic) understanding of the emerging scene. These other features include:

- *Gaze:* the direction of each participant's gaze and how it shifts during interaction.
- *Touch:* self-touch, touching other speakers and touching and manipulating objects and artefacts.
- *Gestures:* actions such as pointing or illustrating a concept.
- *Posture:* orientation of head, shoulders and lower body, and bodily attitude (e.g. direction of lean).

- *Spatial positioning:* where people are in relation to other participants, objects and artefacts.
- *Other actions,* including such things as walking.

Various researchers have developed different ways to make these actions available to readers of transcripts. Your main options are to provide:

- Narrative descriptions of these actions embedded in the discussions of your transcripts.
- Narrative descriptions of these actions embedded in the actual transcripts.
- Specific transcription notation of these actions to be used in the transcripts.
- Line drawings of the actions to be used alongside the transcripts.
- Screen shots of the actions to be used alongside the transcripts.
- Video recordings of the encounters to be used alongside the transcripts.

Again I am going to take a section of the transcript and show how some of these options can be practically achieved. I should note that, due to the complexity of reproducing this work in transcripts, I am only going to take a *very short* section of the transcript and only focus on a few of the features in the ongoing scene.

Transcribing images

The extract below uses both simple transcription (as we saw in Extract 1) and narrative descriptions of the non-verbal actions. Before you read the transcript it is important to get a sense of how everyone is positioned in the space. Tim is standing with his back to Mary and Ben. Tim is facing a hob and keeps tossing the food in the frying pan. Ben and Mary are sitting at a large table, opposite each other.

Extract 1.2 (re-transcribed section of Extract 1)

1		*((Tim looks at Mary))*
2	**Tim**:	Is it all frozen?
3	**Mary**:	No,
4		*((Tim looks at frying pan))*
5	**Mary**:	this part of it's fine. Okay, when you peel it
6		*((Tim glances at Mary and returns gaze to frying pan))*
7	**Ben**:	Uh huh
8	**Mary**:	slice it in four lengthways
9		*((Tim looks at Mary and Ben))*
10	**Ben**:	Oh and then just ((overlap))
11	**Mary**:	a n d t h e n ((overlap)) just take the seeds out
12		*((Tim looks at Ben and points towards him))*
13	**Tim**:	Or alternatively

14		((*Mary looks at Tim and smiles*))
15	**Tim**:	slice it in half
16		((*Mary looks at Ben*))
17	**Tim**:	and use a teaspoon
18		((*Mary throws knife towards Ben*))
19	**Tim**:	and run it along
20	**Mary**:	You can
21		((*Tim turns quickly towards frying pan*))
22		choose whichever method you prefer

As you can see, these narrative descriptions give some sense of life to the scene and some sense of the work that the speakers do. Unfortunately, Ben is off-camera so we only have information on his verbal conduct. What I feel the information adds is that it begins to show you, the reader, just how all these speakers work to co-ordinate their interaction through *both* verbal and non-verbal work. The two are intimately related and without understanding one you cannot fully understand the other. For example, Tim's alternative instructions at 15 – 'slice it in half' – is in direct opposition to Mary's instructions. And note that Tim turns his focus away from the frying pan, towards the other partici-pants, *just after* Mary produces her instruction at 8 – 'slice it in four length-ways' – and then he does not return his focus to the frying pan until just after he has completed offering his alternative version. In this way we can see how her original instructions cue the possibility of alternative instructions and Tim, quite literally, works to fully turn his attention towards the ongoing discussion of how to prepare a cucumber.

To explore this reading further, we can re-present part of the same transcript, but using a more specific form of notation that seeks to mark more precisely where these actions talk place.

Extract 1.3 (re-transcribed section of Extract 1)

1	**Mary**:	=No. this part of it's fine. Okay, when you pee::l it,
		^ ^
	Tim:	*turns* *turns*
		to pan *to Mary*
2	**Ben**:	°Uh huh°
3	**Mary**:	sli:ce it in fou:r.=lengthways (a n d t h e n)
		^ ^
	Tim:	*turns* *rapidly turns*
		to pan *to Mary and Ben*

As you can see, by noting just where Tim turns we can get a better sense of what he is orientating to. And he turns quite rapidly compared to his prior movements, just as Mary is completing the word 'fou:r.', which as we saw is the part of her instruction that Tim later disagrees with – his solution is to slice it in half. So this transcript seeks to demonstrate just where the specific actions take place.

In producing the transcript for Extract 1.3 in that way, I have been able to strengthen my argument. I have provided you, the readers, with what I had access to on the recording. To be sure, a lot more was going on at this moment than I have given you access to in Extract 1.3 above. My *working* transcript for just part of that section looks something like this:

Extract 1.4 (re-transcribed section of Extract 1)

	Mary:	*rocks head from side to side*
		cuts end of cucumber off
		v
1	**Mary:**	**=No.**
		^
	Tim:	*turns to pan and continues to shake pan*
	Mary:	*quickly turns cut end of cucumber*
		towards her and looks at end
		v
2	**Mary:**	**t h i s**
	Mary:	*turns other end of cucumber towards her*
		looks at that end
		v
3	**Mary:**	**part of it's**
	Mary:	*rocks head towards Ben,*
		v
4	**Mary:**	**fine.**
	Mary:	*leans towards Ben*
		raises knife and holds cucumber vertically
		v
5	**Mary:**	**Okay, when**

As you can see, in this version of the transcript I have provided even more detail and I have focused mainly on Mary's work in relation to manipulating the cucumber. The paper version is a lot messier, and takes up about a side of A4, with various arrows and boxes and drawings. And I did not provide this level of detail in Extract 1.3 as it would not add to the specific argument I was trying to build. As a brief aside, you should now be able to see how transcripts can work as rhetorical devices, as the transcript of Extract 1.3 nicely does the work of just arguing my case about how Tim acts. If I added all the work Mary was undertaking, my argument would have been less easily accessible – it would have been lost in these other details.

Another way to give your reader access to what you are seeing is to provide them with screen shots or frame grabs of the video images (see Banks, 2007, in more detail). So rather than just using textual description of actions and gestures, you offer them a visual demonstration. For example, let us re-view in Figure 5.1 the moment when Tim offers his alternative set of instructions on how to prepare cucumbers. So you can now get a sense of some gestural work and bodily orientation of the speakers. Note, for example, how in the first frame Mary is facing Ben (who is off-screen, to the left) and that in frame (b) we can see that she is now looking at Tim and smiling. To produce these images I paused the image on my computer media player at various points and just clicked on 'copy', pasted them in a document and scaled them down. I was using an easily available (and free) media player that I downloaded from the Internet – but note that not all media players give you the option to copy frames.

Through using screen shots, you cannot always show all the fine-grained aspects of movement and gestures. For example, note the difference in how Tim is holding his hands in frames (a) to (e). First, he points towards Ben, then, as he says the words 'slice it in ha::lf,' his left hand moves down in a slicing movement. He then brings his left hand up and positions it as if he is holding something – and given what he is saying 'and use a teaspoon,' this gesture is trying to do the work of demonstrating holding a teaspoon. He then moves his hand forward and up, as if he is scooping something out with this imaginary teaspoon. Now this level of detail about the trajectory of the movement is not always available through the screen shots alone. This is partly due to the speed of the movements alongside the fact that I only use a reasonably basic media player. The point is, irrespective of your technology, short of providing access to the actual recording, some features will always escape (and as I noted above, the recording itself only gives one perspective of the ongoing scene).

One option is to actually provide the recording alongside the text – you can easily burn part of the recording on to a CD-ROM or put part of it onto a website. However, as I noted in the section on ethics, *you must have the approval of the participants* to undertake such things, be it *to reproduce still images, screen shots, sound or video files.* Some researchers will blur out the faces of the participants

(a)

Tim: = **Or alt**ernatively

(b)

Tim: slice it in **ha::lf**,

(c)

Tim: and use a **teaspoon**,

(d)

Tim: ((banging sound)) and run it **along**.

(e)

(0.3)
Mary: **You can** <u>ch</u>oose whichever method you, pre:<u>fer</u>.=

FIGURE 5.1   Re-transcribed section of Extract 1
Note: The text in bold is the point at which the screen shot was taken

69

when reproducing any images or put black boxes over the eyes or faces. Others will reproduce the images through line drawings. As I noted above, there are other ways to render such work, and some people use specific forms of notation to present things like gaze direction or actions on a computer keyboard.

Some closing comments

Once you have generated your audio or video recordings, you generally then want to transform either all or part of those recordings into some form of written document. And I have given you various options as to what level of detail you can provide. In the chapters that follow you will see the different ways that other researchers have produced and used their transcripts and you should be able to get a sense about which version you want to work with, given your specific research questions or interests.

As I have repeatedly mentioned above, through the act of transcription we shape the scene we are trying to describe. In so doing, we shape both our own and the reader's understandings of what is going on in that moment of the interaction and what is important to focus on. The best way to learn how to produce the more detailed transcripts is to transcribe in pairs or better still in a group situation. As you work with others you will debate just why you decided to render that stretch of talk that way. More importantly, such group co-listenings provide a chance to actually undertake some data analysis, where your discussions lead you to re-check your analysis, to re-engage and re-understand just what is going on. A finished transcript should never be the starting point of your analytic work; it is in and through repeated listening or watching your recordings and in and through the ongoing process of transcription that your analysis should be based.

───── Key points

- Your recordings and transcripts are always selective and always partial.
- Try not to undertake all of your analysis from just the transcripts of a recording. Transcripts are living, evolving, documents – they are always susceptible to change and alterations.
- When you start to make detailed transcriptions it can be really helpful to work with someone else, to work jointly on the same recording and help each other out both with what you heard and how to reproduce it on the page.

Further reading

For issues of transcription see also the following resources:

Antaki, C. (2002) *An Introductory Tutorial in Conversation Analysis*. Online at http://www-staff.lboro.ac.uk/~sscal/sitemenu.htm; accessed on 5 Oct. 2005.

Ashmore, M. and Reed, D. (2000) 'Innocence and nostalgia in conversation analysis: the dynamic relations of tape and transcript.' *Forum Qualitative Sozialforschung/Forum: Qualitative Social Research* [Online Journal], 1(3). Online at http://www.qualitative-research.net/fqs-texte/3-00/3-00ashmorereed-e.htm; accessed on 12 Jan 2006.

Banks, M. (2007) *Using Visual Data in Qualitative Research* (Book 5 of *The SAGE Qualitative Research Kit*). London: Sage.

Kvale, S. (2007) *Doing Interviews* (Book 2 of *The SAGE Qualitative Research Kit*). London: Sage.

Poland, B.D. (2002) 'Transcription quality', in J. Gubrium and J. Holstein (eds), *Handbook of Interview Research: Context and Method*. Thousand Oaks, CA: Sage, pp. 629–50.

6
Exploring conversations

Chapter objectives
After reading this chapter, you should

- know more focuses on how you can study talk and conversations;
- see how people, mainly from the research traditions of conversation analysis and discursive psychology, work with audiotapes and videotapes of talk and interaction;
- see, from a discussion of a range of transcripts of talk, some of the key features of talk that people often focus on when analyzing conversations.

At first sight, the idea that studying conversation may be a useful way to make sense of society and culture may seem strange. As part of our everyday life we are bombarded with the obvious truth that talk is 'just talk'. As a child you may have heard the rhyme 'Sticks and stones may break my bones but words can never hurt me'. When we ask someone to account for something they have said they may reply 'Oh well, it is just something I say'. From this perspective, any focus on conversation may appear to be one of the most trivial of things. However, if you stop and think for a moment, it is not hard to see that conversation – or interaction, for want of a more general description – is potentially *the* central way through which we make friends, have relationships, learn things, do our jobs, and so on. As Moerman (1992) explains it, '[T]alk is a central part of social interaction, and social interaction is the core and enforcer, the arena and teacher, the experienced context of social life' (1992, p. 29).

Harvey Sacks, one of the founders of conversation analysis, outlines the central research strategy for conversation analytic work. He 'simply' says: 'Just try to come to terms with how it is that the thing comes off. … Look to see how it is that persons go about producing what they do produce' (1995, Fall 64: 11). To begin to explore Sacks's advice, take the following examples of talk:

Extract 1 (Beach and Metzinger, 1997, p. 569 – simplified transcript)

Sue: Wonder how he found out an all that
           (0.4)
Fiona: I:::: **I don't know** through work or Kay probably

So Sue wonders out loud about how the person known as 'he' found out about something. I take it that most people would hear Fiona as saying 'My *hunch* is that they found out through work or Kay'. Whether Fiona does in fact know but is unwilling to admit this is open to question. However, we can see that she is *displaying* or *doing uncertainty*. In and through the action of displaying or doing uncertainty, Fiona works to say 'Don't hold me accountable for the accuracy of this information'.

Let us view another example of this, taken from a trial for rape. We join the sequence as the defense attorney is cross-examining an alleged rape victim.

Extract 2 (Drew, 1992, pp. 478–9)

Attorney: Well didn't he ask you if uh on that night
                that uh::: he wanted you to be his girl
                (0.5)
Attorney: Didn't he ask you that?
                (2.5)
Witness: **I don't remember** what he said to me that night
                (1.2)
Attorney: Well you had some uh uh fairly lengthy
                conversations with the defendant uh did'n you?
                (0.7)
Attorney: On the evening of February fourteenth?
                (1.0)
Witness: We were all talking.

Again, we can begin to see how the words 'I don't remember' are not necessarily tied to the working of the individual speaker's memory, but rather can be understood as a *social action*. Through the answer 'I don't remember' she avoids confirming the question and so avoids both confirming and disconfirming information that could be potentially damaging or discrediting to her case. The attorney then follows up this line of argument and she answers that '**We** were **all** talking'. In and through displaying her lack of memory or certainty, she displays the lack of importance she gave to the defendant's actions towards her. The defendant's actions, his asking her 'to be his girl' and their 'lengthy conversations', are only unmemorable to her because, at the time, they went unnoticed. The implication is that, at that time, she had no special interest in him or particular reason to notice him; above all she should not be accused of 'leading him on'.

So this style of analysis – often undertaken by people doing conversation analysis and discursive psychology – focuses on *how social actions and practices are accomplished in and through talk and interaction*. As the above examples begin to show, the apparently mundane, trivial or innocent words like 'I don't know', 'probably' and 'I don't remember' do work for participants – they can work to say (among many other things) 'Don't hold me that accountable for what I'm saying'. And this work is *not* tied to individual character, personality or psychology. To be sure, some people might use these words more often than others, but the social action that happens in and through the use of these words, in these specific contexts, is remarkably independent of their individual characteristics.

So one way to explore conversations is to look with wonder at some of the taken-for-granted – seen but unnoticed – ways that we do social life. The aim is to describe the richly layered practices of social life through a close and detailed observation of people's action and interaction. The central sources of these observations are recordings of 'naturally occurring' talk and interaction.

Exploring a mundane moment in talk

In order to explore some of the ways talk can be analyzed, let us focus on another rather 'trivial', ordinary moment of talk.

Extract 3 (Maynard, 1991, p. 461)

1 John: So what do you think about bicycles on campus?
2 Judy: I think they're terrible.
3 John: Sure is about a MILLION of 'em
4 Judy: eh heh

At first glance this might not be that interesting. However, note *how* John works to display his thoughts about bicycles on campus. Rather than just tell Judy what he thinks about them, he asks Judy a question (1). So John *invites* Judy to offer her thoughts or opinions about bicycles. Judy then *replies*, that she thinks 'they're terrible.' (2). Then, and only then, does John report his *perspective*.

So, why should that interest us at all? What we have here is some rather lovely work – these people are actively doing something we all routinely do. We can reproduce the opening lines of their talk as follows:

John invites Judy to talk about a topic (1)

Judy talks about the topic (2)

John then gives his perspective on the same topic and his perspective closely
fits with Judy's (3)

Now, it doesn't take a great leap of imagination to think about a moment when
we all do similar work. Think about the times when you leave the cinema or a
lecture. Often what happens is, rather than say outright 'I hated that film/lec-
ture', you ask the person you are with a question like 'What did you think?' they
then tell you that they 'thought it was excellent', and then you may 'fit' your
response around what they have just said, 'I liked the start but some of it was
quite boring'.

This way of talking, which Maynard (1991) calls the perspective–display
sequence, can be a wonderful way that we *do caution*. Rather than just giving your
opinion 'outright' without knowing whether the other person agrees or not, *once you
have heard their opinion* you can then deliver yours in a 'hospitable environment'
(Maynard, 1991, p. 460) as you can tie what they have said into your own report.

This is one example of how some people, especially conversation analysts and
discursive psychologists, analyze conversations: they focus on *how* speakers
interact. A lot of work has focused on what Heritage (1997) calls 'the social institution *of* interaction' [author's emphasis] (p. 162), *how* everyday interaction, be it
storytelling, disagreeing, answering, and so on, is locally and collaboratively produced. A lot of work also focuses on 'the management of social institutions *in*
interactions' (ibid.), *how* specific institutions, be they law, psychology, family,
education, or whatever, and institutional activities, be they testimony, quality of
life assessment, family meals, lessons, and such like, are locally and collaboratively produced. Discursive psychologists are also focusing on *how* apparently
psychological concepts, like emotion, memory, attitude, and so on, are deeply
social affairs, locally and collaboratively produced in and through action and
interaction rather than just embedded in individuals' cognitions.

The interactional management of diagnosis in a hospital setting

Maynard notes how the perspective–display sequence, which we just saw in
Extract 3 above, can occur when doctors deliver 'bad' diagnostic news. He
recorded some consultations where parents are given a diagnosis about their
child's health.

Extract 4 (Maynard, 1992, p 339 – simplified transcript)

1 **Dr**:   How's Bobby doing.
2 **Mo**: Well he's doing pretty good you know
3   especially in the school. I explained the

75

```
4            teacher what you told me that he might be
5            sent into a special class maybe, that I was
6            not sure. And he says you know I asks his
7            opinion, an' he says that he was doing
8            pretty good in the school, that he was
9            responding you know in uhm everything that
10           he tells them. Now he thinks he's not
11           gonna need to be sent to another school.
12   Dr:     He doesn't think he's gonna need to be
13           sent
14   Mo:     Yeah that he was catching on a little bit uh
15           more you know like I said I- I- I know that
16           he needs a- you know I was 'splaining to her
17           that I'm you know that I know for sure that
18           he needs some special class or something.
19   Dr:     Wu' whatta you think his problem is.
20   Mo:     Speech.
21   Dr:     Yeah. Yeah his main problem is a- you know a
22           language problem
23   Mo:     Yeah language.
```

The doctor asks an open-question about how this mother's child, Bobby, is 'doing'(1). She then replies that he is 'doing pretty good' (2) and goes on to give evidence for this by referring to what Bobby's teacher has been saying (6–11). The doctor then repeats part of the mother's talk (12–13). In the course of reply-ing to his talk, she offers her own opinion – that she knows **'for sure** he needs some special class or something.'(17–18). The doctor then asks another question, *inviting* her to talk about what she thinks is Bobby's '**problem**' (19). She *replies* that it is 'Speech.' (20). Then, and only then, does the doctor report his *per-spective*. He agrees with the Mother's understanding 'Yeah.' (21) and then refor-mulates the problem as 'a **language** problem'(22). She then agrees with this and reformulates her description of the problem in alignment with the doctor's terminology (23). Rather than just offer his perspective at the start of their talk, the doctor delays giving his perspective. Initially the mother just produces 'good' news about her son. She then offers some 'bad' news, which the doctor invites her to elaborate on, which she does. Note how he *only* delivers the 'bad' news diag-nosis once the 'hospitable environment' of 'bad' news talk has been developed. Also, he delivers the 'bad' news diagnosis *as a confirmation* of what the mother already knows. As Maynard notes, a doctor can use a perspective–display sequence to *co-implicate* or *confirm* a parent's view in the delivery of a 'bad' news diagno-sis. In this way, the parent is produced as 'already having some knowledge of their child's condition' and 'good' parents should be experts on their children. Interestingly, the perspective–display sequence can be used by doctors to confirm the parent's own thoughts when they then go on to deliver a diagnosis that is *alternative to* the parent's own thoughts.

Maynard's work also shows us something about one of the methods that conversation analysts and discursive psychologists use. You can *focus on a single episode of talk* to explore in detail how that specific moment of interaction happens. You notice something interesting, something that you think might be an 'organized' way of talking. *You then go and look for other examples*, in other settings, between different speakers to see if you can find other examples of this type of work. In this way, *you attempt to build a case* that this organized way of talking is something that people do as part of their everyday lives – that this thing is part of how we routinely interact.

The routine organization of social life

We can make some further observations about all the extracts given above, which direct us to some of the key features that people often focus on when analyzing conversation.

Turn-taking organization

One of the things to note is how all speakers in the extract given above *take turns at talking*. Think about when you talk to a friend, the talk will often flow in such a way as you speak, they speak, you, them, and so on. And these turns can range from single words, sounds or gestures (like shrugging your shoulders) to long stretches of talk. On such occasions, it is not that you 'can only' or 'always' speak in and through this kind of ordered fashion – you only have to think about all the moments when we interrupt or compete for the floor – but rather this is a routine feature of your talk.

In some encounters the turn-taking organization is *pre-allocated*. Take for example courtrooms or the British House of Commons, where, once in session, only specific individuals can speak at specific times. In courtrooms, the judge determines who is 'out of order', who is in 'contempt of court', and directs others to 'answer the question'. Those not allocated the right to talk should, at all times when in session, be silent witnesses to the proceedings. If they do not perform this action, they can, potentially, be removed or incarcerated. Note how in Extract 2 the pauses after the attorney's questions are hearable as just that witness's pause; given the context, she is responsible for ending that silence over, say, members of the jury. And we can see that after both his questions, when the witness 'fails' to speak, the attorney prompts her to offer an answer to his prior question. However, the social organization of most institutions – be it medicine, gender, academic research or relationships – is not as rigidly fixed and policed in terms of the rights and responsibilities of those involved.

What is also interesting to note is how turn-taking organizations can craft specific rights and responsibilities. When turns are not rigidly pre-allocated, say when you are chatting to your friends over a coffee, as you can never be quite sure when it is your turn – when you might be asked to offer an answer to their question, or make an appreciative sound about a holiday photograph they are talking you through – *you need to listen, you need to be in that moment.* You need to listen so as to know just when to offer that answer or that 'That looks lovely' response. If you are not there, you can be held accountable and then may have to work to repair that potential breach, maybe with a 'Sorry, I was day-dreaming' or 'Sorry, what was that?' In this way, the turn-taking system provides a powerful way to *co-ordinate and display speakers' understanding of the moment.* So by offering the response 'Fine' to your friend's utterance 'How are you?', you can demonstrate that you understood their utterance as a question, and as a question directed at you. If your friend then says, 'I was asking Jim actually', you then understand that that question was not directed at you, and that you are now potentially accountable.

Sequence organization and turn design

In all the extracts above, we could focus on how speakers' specific actions are organized in sequences. It is vital to understand that this style of work *never* just focuses on single sentences or utterances, but rather focuses on *how specific actions* – be they turns of talk or gestures – *are embedded in, emerge from and are understood within the sequences of ongoing actions.* You can think about it like this: our actions are both shaped by prior actions and shape what follows them.

I have already outlined how the talk in Extract 3 demonstrates what Maynard calls a perspective–display sequence. Another massively routine sequence is the *question–answer* sequence, where you ask a question and someone offers an answer. And sequences produce specific courses of action where, given a first action, certain actions are rendered as the preferred next. So when you ask a question you generally expect an answer to just that question. Once you have that answer, you can either start a new sequence, say with another question on a different topic, or follow up the prior answer and so expand that sequence.

What is also important to note is *just how the turns are designed within sequences.* So in Extract 4, the doctor asks a question at 1, the mother offers an answer at 2–11. Her answer is not any old answer. She could have just said 'Well he's doing pretty good you know especially in the school' (2–3) and left it at that, but she actually offers quite an elaborated answer. She tells the doctor that she asked Bobby's teacher about something that this doctor had suggested. This is *potentially* hearable as a criticism of this doctor – maybe she does not have any faith in him? To reduce the potential hearing of criticism, she notes that she was only doing this to 'asks his opinion,' (6–7) – and that is something any good mother would do. To get a sense of how turns are designed you should *focus on the action the talk is designed to perform and the means selected to perform that action* (Drew and Heritage, 1992). In this case, we can see how the mother's turn at 2–10 is designed to show that Bobby is doing well at his current school without overtly contradicting the doctor's prior advice, that Bobby should go to another school. She performs this action through describing a conversation she had with Bobby's teacher that works to position the teacher, rather than her, as suggesting that the doctor may not be right.

The doctor repeats part of her prior talk at 12–13, which follows up on the mother's story about the teacher's reaction, and so implicitly questions that teacher's view. I want to briefly focus on how her turn at 14–18 is designed, and to do this I have reproduced the part of the talk we want to focus on:

Extract 4.1 (section of Extract 4)

```
12  Dr:   He doesn't think he's gonna need to be
13         sent
14  Mo:   Yeah that he was catching on a little bit uh
15         more you know like I said I- I- I know that
16         he needs a- you know I was 'splaining to her
17         that I'm you know that I know for sure that
18         he needs some special class or something.
```

So the mother responds to the doctor's query when she says 'Yeah that he was catching on a little bit uh more' (14–15). What follows works to both answer to the doctor's initial question at 1 and his understanding check at 12–13. She starts this by saying 'I said I- I- I I know that he needs a'(15–16) and then breaks the trajectory of her talk. Given the talk that follows, we can take an educated guess that she was going to say something like 'special class or something'. But what she actually does is considerably more artful. First she explains that 'I was 'splaining to her' (16) and so creates a specific scene: what follows is to be heard as what she actually explained when she was talking to this teacher. And what she told this teacher was not 'I know that Bobby needs a class', but something even more definite than that, 'I know **for sure** that he needs **some** special class or something.' (17–18). So her elaborated answer does some lovely work as it demonstrates that she, unlike the teacher, is aware that Bobby needs some help and so is onside with this doctor's prior view.

Lexical choice and category work

Another feature that analysts focus on is *just what words people use* as they talk. As I have noted in the previous chapters and as my discussion of all the extracts above shows, considering there are multiple possible ways to describe the same person, the same action or the same scene, you need to think what work does it do to use just that word over others. If we focus on Extract 2 above, the transcript of the rape trial, you can see how this is a deeply serious matter. The trial itself is about contested versions of an event and about whether that event can be described as 'rape' or 'consensual sex'. And in Extract 2 we have various contrasting descriptions, including the words:

- 'ask'/'said'
- 'conversations'/'talking'

In both these examples, the first version is the attorney's (ask, conversations) and the second version is the witness's, and in both cases the witness's version is a less specific, more general, descriptor. Think of the difference between saying:

- 'I don't remember what he *asked me* that night' and
- 'I don't remember what he *said to me* that night'

The first version positions her as potentially remembering some features of their talk; she may not remember what he asked her, but maybe she did remember some of other things they talked about. The second version, the one she actually gives in answer to his question, works to say I can't remember *any* of details of what we talked about.

Structural organization

The organization of 'structure' refers to *just how the broader trajectory of the talk is organized*. For example, if you think about phone conversations you have with friends, you may often have experienced the following structure of sequences:

- Opening – where you say your hellos and sometimes have to work out just who is talking and whether that is the person you wanted to speak to.
- Reason for the call – where you introduce the reason for the chat, be it 'I just though I'd phone because I hadn't spoken to you for ages' to 'Did you hear about Tim?'
- Discussion of topic that was the reason for the call – which may or may not go on for some time.
- New topic emerges – this may or may not happen.
- Discussion of new topic.
- Close – where you say your goodbyes.

Again, it is not that all phone conversations with friends go this way, but rather this sort of trajectory is something we are familiar with and work with and against with each new phone call. And with some friends it may be that you just know it is really hard to close calls and that even when you have said your 'See you later' or 'It was really nice to speak again', they work to reopen that conversation, and maybe you have developed certain solutions.

So as you start analyzing *how* a stretch of talk is locally and collaboratively produced, focusing on some of these features I have outlined may help you get a sense of the work the speakers are massively and routinely engaged in. Whenever I overhear other people's conversations, or sit back and listen as conversations I am involved in evolve, or listen to or watch recordings I have made, I find that I am fascinated and constantly amazed by the kind of work we do when we interact with others. By just thinking about how some of the above features of talk work in relation to your own experiences and recordings, you can become *more sensitive* to just how that specific interaction 'comes off'. I need to stress that the above list of things to focus on should *not* be read as a recipe that you should follow as you engage with your research topic, but rather was given to provide some access points to things you may want to focus on when analyzing conversations you have collected.

I am now going to focus on two other routine organizations of social life: the organization of agreement and disagreement, and a feature of storytelling. I am focusing on these both to explore the topics themselves as well to give you access to two contrasting ways of how you can present data and build an argument. One of them appears as rather technical and relies heavily on gathering many different cases and extracts, whereas the other one focuses on just one extract.

An observation on an aspect of storytelling

Below is an extended extract taken from Sacks' (1995) work. The talk begins where Agnes is asking about a house that Portia recently visited.

Agnes: I bet it's a dream, with the swimming pool enclosed huh?

Portia: Oh God, we hehh! we swam in the nude Sunday night until about two o'clock.

Now what I take it that 'hehh!' is doing, and what I take it a bunch of 'hehh's are doing is something like this: Something is about to be reported which the teller takes it that the hearer should know what the teller's attitude towards it is. The kind of event being reported could be specifically equivocal as to whether it is something awful, embarrassing, serious, non-serious, etc. And there are ways for the teller to let the recipient know which the teller thinks it is, so as to guide the recipient in figuring out things about the teller's participation. So, for example, in the report about swimming in the nude, by using 'hehh!' before reporting it she's saying 'I took it lightly.' Where it could be read as a kind of obscene event, it is rather to be treated as something light-hearted. It was funny. Where it perhaps could be important for the teller to have the recipient know or believe that the teller thought it was that sort of thing. (1995, Spring 1970, 7: 275)

The talk, and the analysis that follows, clearly shows us how just a single utterance placed early in a story does a lot of work for *both* speakers.

Now in this sequence of talk Portia is producing a report. Note how Sacks tells us that the event reported could be 'specifically equivocal' and that Portia works to 'guide' Agnes as to how to hear what she thought about it. So in this way, the 'hehh!' does a lot of work for Portia:

- It *'fixes' or 'guides'* how the report is to be heard, as a 'report of something funny and not as a report of something obscene or embarrassing or serious etc.' In this way it produces the talk that follows as a specific kind of talk. It also produces her talk as a 'tellable story'.
- In forecasting that the talk that follows is to be heard as chuckleable talk, it makes relevant that the preferred response is to attend to it as chuckleable talk. Having recognized that the talk has finished, the preference is that Agnes should then produce something hearable as 'doing chuckleability'.
- In forecasting the talk as 'chuckleable talk', Portia has constructed a specific identity in relation to the talk that follows. She has produced herself as 'someone who finds swimming in the nude as unproblematic'. But note that she produces this as unproblematic in reference to this specific speaker at this specific moment; it is not produced as unproblematic per se. As such the preface works to explicitly deny the relevance of other possible identities.

And what makes this action of prefacing quite interesting is its 'simplicity', in this case it was but a single laughter token. And Sacks's observation is utterly simple and yet, for me, utterly convincing. The strength of his argument is not in presenting a whole series of cases but rather through *exploring in detail just this case*. And his observation about just this case can be extended to other moments in interaction. We can easily think about the ways that people provide others with such contextual information – be it through laughter, gestures or words – about how to hear and understand what they are saying.

Some observations on the social institution of refusal and disagreement

A considerable body of work has been undertaken that collects together many instances of talk where people are either accepting or refusing something, be it an invitation, offers, requests, proposals (Davidson, 1984; Drew, 1984), or agreeing or disagreeing with assessments (Pomerantz, 1984). They have documented the routine ways that people do acceptance and refusal and agreement and disagreement in Anglo-American talk. First, let us focus on some examples of agreement and acceptance.

Extract 5 (Davidson, 1984, p. 116 – simplified transcript)

A: Well, will you help me (out
B: (**I certainly will**

Extract 6 (Pomerantz, 1984, p. 60)

J: It's really a clear lake, isn't it?
R: **It's wonderful**

As you can see, acceptance (Extract 5) and agreement (Extract 6) are routinely done immediately, with no gap in the talk (and sometimes overlapping the other speaker's talk) and are relatively 'forthright', in that they are simple and straightforward. Compare this to how refusals and disagreements are often produced.

Extract 7 (Pomerantz, 1984, p. 101)

B: Wanna comne down 'n have a bite a' <u>lunch</u> with me?
      I got some beer en stuff.
A: **Wul yer real <u>sweet</u> hon, uhm, let-=**
B: (D'you have sumpn else?
A: (I have-
A: **No, I have to uh call Bill's mother**

Extract 8 (Heritage, 1984, p. 271)

((S's wife has just slipped a disk))
H: And we were <u>w</u>ondering if there's <u>a</u>nything we can do to help
S: (**Well 'at's**
H: (I mean can we do any shopping for her or
      Something like tha:t?
      (0.7)
S: **Well that's <u>most</u> kind Heather<u>ton</u> .hhh**
      At the moment <u>no</u>:. because we've still got the bo:ys at home.

Extract 9 (Pomerantz, 1984 p. 73)

B: I think I'll call her and ask her if she's
      interested because she's a good nurse, and I
      think they would like her don't you?
A: **Well, I'll tell you, I haven't seen Mary for**
      <u>years.</u> I should- As I remember, yes.
B: Well do you think she would fit in?
A: **Uhm, uh, I don't know, What I'm uh**
      hesitating about is uh – – uhm maybe she would.
      (1.0)
A: **Uh but I would hesitate to uhm – –**

The difference is clear. With a refusal or disagreement you routinely get some combination of the following actions:

- *Delays*: a gap before a response or a gap within a response, a delay before an answer is given.
- *Hesitations*: like 'mm' 'erm' 'uhm' and in-breath or out-breaths.
- *Prefaces*: like 'Well' and 'Uh', agreement tokens like 'Yeah'.
- *Mitigations*: apologies and appreciations.
- *Accounts*: excuses, explanations, justifications and reasons.

Interestingly, a lot of the time we say 'no' without ever explicitly saying it and other speakers understand us to be saying 'no' without ever having to hear us say it out loud.

Researchers have documented how we can 'notice' a potential or upcoming refusal or disagreement prior to someone actually producing one. For instance, in Extract 10 below, note how speaker Z works to make their invitation more 'inviting':

Example 10 (Davidson, 1984 p. 105 – simplified transcript)

Z: C'mon down here,=it's okay
     (0.2)
Z: I got lotta stuff,=I got beer and stuff 'n

Even after the micro-pause (around two-tenths of a second), Z works to upgrade their invitation with the 'sweetener' of providing 'beer and stuff'. In this case, Z has heard this pause as a potential refusal and shows the other speaker (and us) what she has taken it to mean. We have seen related work in Extract 7 above. Just after A's appreciative comment 'Wul yer real <u>sweet</u> hon, uhm, let-=', B asks the question 'D'you have sumpn else?' B's question marks that they have heard A's talk as a preface to an upcoming rejection of the invitation. So we are able to monitor other people's talk for the finest of distinctions.

Through such *detailed comparative analysis* of instances of talk, conversation analysts have outlined how the work of agreeing/accepting and disagreeing/refusing is routinely done. This is not to say they we all behave like robots and that this is *the only* way that people do this work, but rather, when doing sociality we routinely work with and against this specific normative interaction order. You only have to think of the multiple ways that a quick and plain 'no' can be orientated to as producing the speaker as blunt or rude, as someone who holds a heartfelt opinion on that specific topic or as someone who is being mischievous. Also, in some cases, a quick and plain 'no' may be the preferred response, say for example when someone makes the self-assessment 'My new haircut makes me look terrible'.

These two alternative, but non-equivalent, courses of actions – preferred actions that are direct and plain responses and dispreferred actions that are delayed and embellished responses – document what conversation analysts call *preference organization*. Their concept of 'preference' does not refer to inner psychological or subjective experiences of individual speakers. Rather it describes one of the systematic ways that speakers in general, *across a range of actions, contexts and situations*, work to organize the social institution of talk and interaction.

So what?

You may have asked yourself, having read how refusal and acceptance is interactionally completed, so what? Well, for some the answer is: it is just fascinating in its own right. For others, this may not be enough. I want to briefly introduce an example of some work that shows the potential insights that can be gained from a detailed focus on *what people actually do*, rather than what we imagine they might or should do.

Kitzinger and Firth (1999) have taken the observation that in Anglo-American interaction there 'is an organized and normative way of doing indirect refusal' (1999, p. 310) and *taken this observation very seriously*. They have begun to question the 'refusal skills' training advocated by many date-rape prevention programmes. As was outlined above, as part of our everyday lives, we routinely understand and orientate to people saying 'no' without them ever having to necessarily say 'no' out loud. Kitzinger and Firth suggest that

> the insistence of date rape prevention (and other refusals skills) educators on the importance of saying 'no' is counter-productive in that it demands that women engage in conversationally abnormal actions which breach conventional social etiquette, and in allowing rapists to persist with the claim that if a woman has not actually said 'NO' (in the right tone of voice, with the right body language, at the right time) then she hasn't refused to have sex with him. (1999, p. 310)

As they outline, for a man to claim that because the women didn't actually say 'no', he 'just didn't understand' or 'wasn't clear whether' she was refusing sex, produces him as socially ignorant and interactionally incompetent. It is not that these men are cultural dopes, or that these men just do not understand 'women's ways' of communicating; rather these men do not like being refused sex. As the authors note, '[t]he problem of sexual coercion cannot be fixed by changing the way women talk' (1999, p. 311).

85

Some closing comments

When you are undertaking such fine-grained analysis you are constantly preoc-
cupied with describing the *lived work* of talking and interacting. Doing such
analysis can begin to show that the work of being an ordinary member of society
is made up of masses of tacit, taken-for-granted, knowledges and practices. Such
an approach is not going to be for everyone, as it often produces rather modest,
descriptive, claims about things we all already just know 'at a glance'. What we
can all take away from these types of investigations is that talk is not just a 'trivial' medium for social life, but rather it is *in and through* our talk and interactions
that we experience, produce and maintain social life. As Sacks notes:

> (I)n every moment of talk, people are experiencing and producing their
> cultures, their roles, their personalities. ... (Y)ou and I live lives of talk,
> experience the social world as motivated talkers and listeners, as
> tongued creatures of the social order; each with our own bursts of pleas-
> ure and pain, each with our proud differences of personal style. (Cited
> in Moerman, 1988, p. xi)

▤ Key points

- People doing conversation analysis and discursive psychology often
  focus on how social actions and practices are accomplished in and
  through talk and interaction.
- They often focus on features of interaction like: how speakers take turns
  at talk; how talk is shaped by prior actions and shapes what follows it;
  how talk is designed to perform certain actions; what words people
  use; and how the broader trajectory of talk is organized.
- They sometimes do detailed analysis of single cases of talk. They also collect and compare similar instances of talk to identify some of the systematic ways that speakers in general, across a range of actions, contexts
  and situations, work to organize the social institution of talk and interaction.

Further reading

Here you will find some more information about the analytic styles discussed in
this chapter:

Hepburn, A. and Potter, J. (2003). 'Discourse analytic practice', in C. Seale,
  D. Silverman, J. Gubrium and G. Gobo (eds), *Qualitative Research Practice*.
  London: Sage, pp. 180–96.
Silverman, D. (1998) *Harvey Sacks: Social Science and Conversation Analysis*.
  Cambridge: Polity Press.
ten Have, P. (1999) *Doing Conversation Analysis: A Practical Guide*. London: Sage.

7
Exploring conversations about and with documents

Chapter objectives
After reading this chapter, you should

- see how documents, and other 'non-human things' (like pens or computers), co-ordinate and produce peoples'. actions and interactions;
- know more about the previous chapter's discussion on how to study talk from three case studies; and
- see how a detailed analysis of moments of talk can say something about the 'big' structures and institutions of social life.

This chapter focuses on a reasonably under-researched area of social life: the role of documents and texts in our everyday life and the various institutions we engage with. You only have to think about the sheer volume of paper and electronic-based documents that you have to engage with on a day-to-day basis to get a sense of how they are a central organizing device in our contemporary cultures. In this chapter I want to briefly explore just a few ways to analyze *how documents and texts are created, used and spoken for in various contexts.* And I am not going to focus on documents or texts in an abstract way, but rather *people's local and collaborative in situ work and interaction with and on documents.*

Documents-in-use

As I speak about 'documents' and 'texts' I am using these terms in their broadest sense to refer to the whole range of written and visual documents we read, use and engage with as part of our everyday lives. I am thinking of things like the chalk board or hand-sized laminated coffee menu you read in your local café to the computer screen of the telephone salesperson with its script and mouse-click options menu to the handwritten notes you prepare and re-read frantically just prior to entering the exam room.

We never just somehow neutrally or abstractly engage with documents, they are always engaged with in a specific *local context*; as such, they are always read or used in a specific way, to do specific work. For example, if you think about this document, you could ask the following research questions:

- How are you reading this document at this moment?
- Are you taking notes on a separate piece of paper?
- How do your notes relate to and transform the text?
- Is this a photocopy or the book?
- Do you read sections of it out loud to others?
- How do you introduce and close the sections you read out?
- Where are you reading this?
- Are you doing this in the library?
- With friends?
- In a seminar?

So when thinking about documents-in-use you should focus on questions about the immediate here-and-now context – questions about the immediate setting, the people and the evolving situation.

When it comes to researching other people's document use, you would only be able to answer such questions with some ethnographic knowledge of that context – by observing and/or informally or formally interviewing the participants – alongside video- or audio-based recordings. You may also need to follow the specific document as it moves from space to space or between people. You may need to ask questions about how it is central to different tasks in different situations. For example, if I think about one book I own, a reasonably obscure academic text, it is interesting to think about the biography of Tim-and-that-book, the kinds of actions and interactions that have been produced in and through me owning just that book. In relation to just that book, here are a few of the encounters that have emerged where that book has been relevant to the interaction:

> Sitting in a café, I have searched through the book and read out specific passages to explain to friends just how this book is written in an obscure academic language – which made them laugh and prompted

a discussion about the different purposes that 'social science' and 'science' books are written for.

Sitting outside a café, during the middle of a conversation about the differences and similarities between certain key social theorists, I have read out passages from that book to stand as evidence for the type of academic work I am interested in pursuing and why it is different from other types of theory.

Whilst going for a walk into town, I have quoted, from memory, certain phrases from the book and summarized other sections of it, in order to explain to a friend why that book is useful to read and what kind of styles of thinking it can lead to.

I have been reading it, whilst sitting on my own outside my favourite café, to pass the time before I meet a friend, and a stranger has asked me 'Is the book interesting?' This opening conversational move led to a lengthy discussion about what it is like to live in the city we live in.

So as you can see, this is the same book and it has featured in a range of encounters and been part of different work in each of those encounters.

A focus on documents-in-use also enables a focus on what some researchers have called 'material culture' or 'the social life of objects'. It can raise your awareness about how 'things', be they books, asthma inhalers or wheelchairs, are embedded in and intimately transform our actions and interactions. Again, if you think about this document, you could ask the following research questions:

- Are you reading this with a pen or pencil in your hand?
- Are you underlining words?
- Do you read differently with a pen or pencil?
- Do you read differently, or treat the document differently, when it is a photocopy?
- How does a photocopy change your reading?
- How did that photocopy get made?
- Do some photocopiers make you angry, say when some of the words or page numbers are lost?
- How did you learn to get the best results from that photocopier?

So, by not only focusing on the people and situation surrounding you, but also the so-called material culture – the things, technologies, artefacts, built environment – you can see how this is part of, and central to, just what it is that people do and say. In this sense, you can *see how documents* (whether paper or computer-based) *and related technologies* (of bookmarks, pens, highlighters, photocopiers, computers, printers etc) *both constrain and enable our actions and interactions.* Above all they are routinely central to the trajectory of our actions with documents. **89**

Again, to study such things you will probably need some ethnographic knowledge alongside any audio or video recordings.

Finally, a focus on documents-in-use can raise questions about how our actions and interactions are embedded in and produce *broader, extra-local, contexts and structures*. So again, in relation to just this document, you could ask:

- What course is this document part of?
- How is it that qualitative research is seen as valuable in some courses/disciplines and not others?
- How is it that knowing about research technique is increasingly seen by the state as more important than knowledge about theory?
- Does the fact that you are reading this, say in a seminar group consisting of fifteen people, reflect a particular trajectory of the funding of the academy?
- Why are you reading this document?
- Did you read the back cover and the reviews from 'leading authors' in the field?
- How is it that the reviewers and those reviewers' comments are chosen?
- How is it that academic publishing works?
- How is it that certain books and topics are commissioned and promoted more than others?

Such a style of questions may lead your analysis beyond the immediate here and now of the actions and interactions you are observing. It may lead you to collect, study and interrogate other documents that outline the history, politics and trajectory of specific institutions. But you may also use ethnographic and audio or video data to show how specific institutions – say gender, therapy or education – are (re)produced at the very moment that the document gets talked about or used.

In order to begin to explore how you could undertake work that can look at features like the materiality of documents and the immediate and broader contexts, I am going to offer a few examples of work that focuses on some versions of documents-in-use.

Case study: How a psychiatric record was created

Tony Hak (1992, 1998) has written several papers that focus on how a specific document and related courses of action were locally, temporally and collaboratively produced. In a range of articles he follows a series of encounters between staff from a psychiatric service and a patient, Anna-Lize. His dataset consisted of the following sources:

1. A paper copy of a psychiatric case report that was made by a nurse after an initial interview with Anna-Lize.
2. An audiotape and transcript of a staff member's home visit and interview with Anna-Lize and her parents.
3. An audiotape and transcript of the staff member's telephone consultation with staff at the hospital to discuss the possibility of admitting Anna-Lize.
4. An audiotape and transcript of an interview with Anna-Lize conducted at the crisis intervention centre.
5. An audiotape and transcript of the staff member's discussion with a colleague at the crisis intervention centre.
6. A paper copy of the second psychiatric case report made by the staff member. (Source: Modified version of Hak, 1992, p. 148.)

As you can see, Hak had access to data that gave him an insight into both some of the documentation of the case and a range of interviews and conversations. He was therefore able to follow the trajectory of the case and see how and to what extent the second psychiatric case report related to those interviews and conversation and to the first case report.

In the papers he has written, Hak gives the readers access to both the case reports and parts of the transcripts of the interviews with Anna-Lize and her family. Below, I have reproduced part of the second case report:

> It is obvious that the client has delusions. She fancies that her sexual past is being disclosed on the radio. And that her father can hear her all the time as well. On the other hand, she frequently hears voices. She seems to hear the voice of her father, even when he is not present. It is not clear to me what extent these are hallucinations. (Second case report: Hak, 1992, p. 154)

He also gives the reader access to the following fragments of the interview and puts them alongside the sections of the second report. Note that SM refers to the staff member and AL refers to Anne-Lize, the patient:

Extract 1 (Hak, 1992, pp. 149–50 – slightly modified transcript)

Interview at home	Second case report
(Fragment 1)	

AL: I've just been used all my life.
SM: By whom?
AL: By boys.
SM: And how does the whole country know about this?
AL: Yes, it is broadcast.
SM: Broadcast where? On the radio or something?
AL: And on TV.

SM:	That you're being used?	**She fancies that her sexual past**
AL:	No un who I went to bed with.	**Is being disclosed on the radio**

	(Fragment 2)	
AL:	My dad also hears every move I make upstairs	**(She fancies) that her father can hear her all the time as well. She seems to hear the voice of her father even when he is not present**

	(Fragment 3)	
AL:	When I suddenly heard voices, I went completely crazy	**On the other hand, she frequently hears voices.**

As you can see, even with this very short extract, Anne-Lize's and the staff members' talk gets transformed in the second document. Her descriptions of her situation are reformulated and are reproduced as an official, factual, version of Anne-Lize. Note, for example, what is both present and absent in the second case report. Her description that 'I've been used all my life' does not appear in the second case report (or the first). Also, that for her, 'who I went to bed with' is being broadcast on the radio 'and on TV' is transformed into 'She fancies that her **sexual past** is being disclosed **on the radio**'.

As Hak notes, if you just had access to the case reports you could do some work on how this patient is described and the language of case reports, you could do some work on how such documents order the information so as to make a case. If you just had access to the interview, you could do some work on how psychiatric staff interact with patients and look at what sorts of questions are relevant to psychiatric assessment and how they structure and direct such interviews. However, in having access to the whole range of encounters and documents, you can learn a lot more about this service. You can see just how, over a course of encounters, Anne-Lize is produced as a relevant patient for psychiatric care and, more importantly, how the encounters and the case reports relate to each other. In so doing you can get a sense of the practices of psychiatry – how psychiatry works to transform patients' actions into psychiatric findings and how they diagnose conditions. In such a way, Hak's approach gives the reader access to some of the ways that the field of psychiatry knows, understands and categorizes patients.

Case study: Reading from and reporting findings of a report

Another way to think about documents-in-use is to focus on how documents get referred to and quoted from in an interaction. Jenkings and Barber (2004, 2006) undertook a study of Hospital Drug and Therapeutic Committees (DTC) meetings and focused on the role of documents in those meetings. The role of DTCs is to control which of the new drugs will be available in a specific hospital and in some cases restrict drug usage to specific medical teams or reject their use in the specific hospital. Some of these drugs cost a lot of money, so the DTC has to make decisions about whether including this drug is cost-effective. Document use is important in this process as the committee, in part, needs to base its decisions on published research evidence about the clinical and cost effectiveness of the drugs.

The data consisted of observing and audiotaping four consecutive meetings of two different DTCs. In addition, they also obtained all the documentation that was prepared for each meeting. This was important as in some meetings one of the participants would often prepare a summary report of the research evidence on a specific drug, in others the participants would have been expected to have read pre-circulated research papers.

One of Jenkings and Barber's interests was in how these written reports were transformed (or not) when they were read out. For example, note how the relatively simple statement in the text, '4) Dose of Aspirin was 325mg', is transformed as it is read out by the pharmacist:

Extract 2 (Jenkings and Barber, 2006,
p. 180 – slightly modified transcript)

Pharmacist: The other thing about it is the **dose of Aspirin** used is **325**
Chair: Which is much higher (.)
Pharmacist: Higher than I think most people have (.) there is a list there of the incidence of the side effects

Note how in reproducing the textual statement it is *tailored to the local context of their talk*. The pharmacist uses the phrase 'the other thing about it' prior to offering the fact. In this way they raise this issue as potentially relevant to this DTC work. And the chair of the DTC collaborates in this act of noticing, or highlighting, and makes the evaluation that this dosage level 'is much higher'. The pharmacist then extends and confirms the chair's evaluation. So in this way, a fact about this drug is situated in this DTC 'world of what we usually do' and so a potentially negative evaluation is being made.

We can see similar work – of situating and transforming texts – if we compare a section of the report with how the pharmacist presents that report.

Summary Report (Jenkings and Barber,
2006, p. 181)

Considerations
1. Consultant only prescription.
2. Not recommended in unstable angina.

93

3. No safety data on concomitant use with Aspirin.
4. Not recommended to be used with Warfarin.
5. May be preferable to Ticlopidine which causes neutropenia (3%) and is unlicensed.
6. For use only in patients intolerant or fail on Aspirin. Not first line in view of very little benefit for huge increase in expenditure.
7. How do we define intolerant?

Extract 3 (Jenkings and Barber, 2006, p. 181– slightly modified transcript)

Pharmacist : **They have said that it should be** consultant prescription (.) **it is** not recommended in unstable angina (.) **there is** no safety data **at all** on concomitant use of Aspirin **which I think is an area where they might want to use it** (.) **it is** not recommended **with** Warfarin (.) **it** may be preferable to the Ticlopidine **that is sometimes used which** is unlicensed which **does** cause neutropenia **which is obviously (unclear) and erm** (.) **I would think that it should** only be used in patients **who are** intolerant or fail on Aspirin **and obviously** not first line **because it is going to be a** huge increase **in costs for everybody if they all change over to this** (.) **and I think my main question was** how do you define intolerant (2.0) **because you know its a bit open ended** (.)

The text given in bold in Extract 3 marks the words that the pharmacist uses that are additional to the original summary report. If you compare the two you can see how the pharmacist provides a lot of *contextual information* about just how to understand the information he is providing. Note how they work to offer a specific version of their concerns about this specific drug. For example, they say that there is 'no safety data **at all**', which adds an extra level of potential concern compared to the summary report's version 'no safety data'. Similarly, point 7 in the summary report is prefaced as '**my main question**' and then followed by the phrase '**because you know its a bit open ended**' that upgrades their potential concern.

So this work begins to show just how texts are transformed in and through the actions of reading them out. This is not to say that it should be any other way, or to expressly criticize that pharmacist's actions; such contextualizing work is a routine feature of how we read things out. The point is to understand how texts, when read out from or quoted verbatim, are tailored to the local situation and context. This tailoring work, whether it be introducing what you are about to read, adding comments as you are reading from a text, or your talk that follows once you have read something out, does work. In this process, the textual description is transformed and tailored to just that audience. Jenkings and Barber's work also shows us how DTCs operate, how they work with and transform research evidence in the very moments they draw on and use that research evidence. Considering that all aspects of contemporary health care (and beyond) are becoming increasingly 'evidence-based' – where high-quality research evidence from randomized controlled trials and other rigorous methods is apparently neutral, stable and transferable – these authors add yet more questions about the plausibility of this vision. As they show, for practitioners, research evidence is always – and has to be – tailored to the specifics of the locations it is to be implemented in.

Case study: Making sense of a video recording in courtrooms

Goodwin (1994a) undertook an analysis of the Rodney King trial. Four White-American police officers had stopped King, an African-American, and then physically assaulted the man. Unknown to the officers, a man across the street had made a videotape of the incident. One of the things that Goodwin's analysis highlights is how texts – albeit in this case a video recording – do not speak for themselves but rather that they are always *spoken for*. In the case of the Rodney King trial, the defense and the expert police witness collaborated in producing a specific way to make sense of the images on the tape. Throughout the trial, the defense argued that the videotape was an objective record of the incident and used the testimony produced with a range of expert witnesses to instruct the jury to understand the video of the beating of King as an example of 'good' police work. The defense argued, successfully in the first court case, that the video displayed that the officers were *only* engaged in 'careful, systematic police work' (1994a, p. 617).

Goodwin's analysis was based on video recordings he made of the trial from broadcasts that appeared on 'Court TV'. How to 'make sense' of the video record of the police officers' and Rodney King's actions became a central feature of the trial. Extract 4 below is a transcript from part of the defense's case. We join the talk as the videotape of the incident is being played, stopped and commented on.

Extract 4 (Goodwin, 1994a, p. 617 – slightly modified transcript)

```
1  Defense:  Four oh five, oh one.
2            We see a blow being delivered=
3            = Is that correct.
4  Expert:   That's correct.
5            The-force has again been escalated (0.3)
6            To the level it had been previously, (0.4)
7            And the de-escalation has ceased.
              ...
8  Defense:  And at-
```

95

9		At this point which is,
10		for the record four thirteen twenty nine, (0.4)
11		We see a blow being struck
12		and thus the end of a period of, de-escalation?
13		Is that correct Captain.
14	Expert:	That's correct.
15		Force has now been elevated to the previous level, (0.6)
16		After this period of de-escalation.

This small fragment contains two sequences (1–7 and 8–16) that share very similar features: the defense does some description then asks a question about that description, and the expert witness answers that question and in so doing produces some re-description. What is important to note is how, through their actions, they collaborate to build a way of how to 'make sense' of the images on the video.

With the first sequence, the defense lawyer calls out the time of the image 'Four oh five, oh one.' (1) and then describes the image 'We see **a blow** being delivered=' (2). Note how he describes the action in the image: this is to be seen and understood as a single blow, this is not a beating or an attack. He then asks for confirmation of his description, '=Is that correct.' (3). The expert witness confirms this (4) and then re-describes the action in the image. This is not to be seen only as a 'blow', but as a moment when 'The- **force** has again **been escalated** … the **de-escalation has ceased**. ' (5–7). With this re-description, the single image of the blow is now to be seen as a precise moment of 'escalation' to a precise 'level' (6) of force. With the second sequence (8–14) similar work goes on, except that in this sequence the defense lawyer also uses the description 'the end of a period of, de-escalation' (12) to account for the police officers' actions.

In this example, the defense case works around coding and highlighting each of the blows on the video ('Four oh five, oh one.' and 'four thirteen twenty nine') as separate, distinct, actions. The forty-seven strikes to Rodney King's body, which happen moments apart, are transformed by the interaction between the defense lawyer and the police expert as separate, distinct uses of force. This 'individual' strike is *only* to be understood as a moment of elevation or escalation of force, a moment when the period of de-escalation has ceased. The moments between blows are to be understood as 'an assessment period' (Goodwin, 1994a, p. 617) where the officers are analyzing Rodney King's actions for signs of co-operation. As the defense went on to argue, 'Rodney King and Rodney King alone was in control of the situation' (ibid, p. 618).

The defense argument was enabled, in part, by the technology of video players, that you could literally pause the action at specific points and so reproduce these actions as individual actions. When talking through the videos they used pointers to further dissect and further focus the jury's attention on the micro-movements of King and the officers. They also produced photographs from the video – close-ups of specific frames were enlarged and cropped – and then directed the jury's viewing through overlaying clear sheets with lines, again re-focusing the jury's vision and knowledge. In this way, this co-ordination of talk and technologies mutually elaborated a specific way to make sense of the emerging scene. Through Goodwin's analysis (and I have only set out a very small part of his work) we can begin to grasp how seeing and knowing are not simply a product of inner psychological processes but rather intimately tied to complex local and situated social actions and interactions. And the authority to see, know and tell is intimately tied to specific professions and as such is unevenly distributed.

Some closing comments

With my brief tour of how people create, use and speak for documents, I have tried to offer you some technical access to the kinds of source materials people use and how they have attempted to ask questions about their materials. These source materials have all included audio and/or video recordings of naturally occurring interactions and in some cases field observations and collecting copies of the documents that the participants are using, creating or talking about. What is central to this work, and a key analytic question, is just how documents or texts are part of the emerging encounter. The point is to take seriously and focus on the potential work of documents – and other elements of material culture – in co-ordinating and producing people's actions and interactions.

As you begin to ask questions about the local and collaborative work of people and non-human 'things', you can also begin to understand how they are embedded in and reproduce, again and again, with each moment, so-called broader contexts and institutions, like psychiatry, medicine or law. As the examples from this and the prior chapter begin to show, the focus is on *how* institutions are produced in and through the collaborative actions and interactions of people and things. So what the analysis of conversation allows us to do is to try to document the ways that people and things organize specific institutions and institutional tasks and identities. In this way, you can develop an analytic understanding of the various institutions of social life that is based on what, at times, goes on in these institutions rather than on a priori assumptions about what you think 'should be' going on. *Only* conducting interviews or focus group with participants about what they do or *only* reading texts that describe what participants do, will only ever offer part of that story and will often miss the quite beautiful, sophisticated and artful ways that we reproduce social life.

═══ Key points

- We never just somehow neutrally or abstractly engage with documents, they are always engaged with in a specific local context; as such, they are always read or used in a specific way, to do specific work.

- Documents – whether paper or computer-based – alongside the vast array of objects we encounter in our day-to-day life, are central to co-ordinating, constraining and enabling our actions and interactions.
- Studies of how documents – and other objects and technologies – feature in and are used in mundane interactions can help us throw a new light on how the structures and institutions of social life, such as psychiatry, medicine and law, are produced, organized and sustained.

Further reading

In these sources, you will find more examples of the analytic work outlined in this chapter:

Livingston, E. (1987) *Making Sense of Ethnomethodology*. London: Routledge & Kegan Paul, chap. 15.
Prior, L. (2003) *Using Documents in Social Research*. London: Sage
Smith, D.E. (1990) *Texts, Facts and Femininity: Exploring the Relations of Ruling*. London: Routledge, chap. 3.

8
Exploring conversations and discourse: some debates and dilemmas

Chapter objectives
After reading this chapter, you should

- see some of dilemmas that you can face when you study conversations and discourse;
- know more on how best to understand and work with interview or focus group data;
- be aware of what your role is in making claims about what is going on in your data; and
- see what a detailed analysis of a small section of talk can really say about things like 'power'.

The previous two chapters have begun to explore how you can undertake a detailed analysis of conversations and documents-in-use. Unsurprisingly, the approaches, techniques and ideas I have outlined are not without their critics. Much of the critique centres on how this style of work either *misses* or *just refuses to engage* with the broader contexts and structures that are the mainstay of many social scientists' work. I am thinking about concepts such as 'power' or 'inequality'. As one person noted to me, 'It feels like people are too obsessed with the detail and just don't look up from the transcripts, they don't notice what is *really* going on in the world'.

Van Dijk (1999) describes the two positions that those who study discourse can find themselves in. On the one hand, these are those analysts who are not afraid to make use of their social knowledge that being black, being a woman, being young or being the boss will most likely be evident from the way people write and talk. In other words, they assume that discourse may reproduce social inequality. (1999, p. 460)

The counter-claim, made by another group of analysts, is that

such an approach should not merely presuppose (even plausible) contextualisation, but 'prove' it by attending to the details of what social members actually say and do. If not, contextualisation is pointless because of its discursive irrelevance. (1999, p. 460)

This debate centres on these two opposing and often overly idealized positions. To unpack this debate, let us re-focus on part of an interaction we saw earlier, 'the politics of cucumbers' kitchen discussion. I have reproduced part of the extract below:

Extract 1 (the politics of cucumbers: Kitchen10: 2.17–3.17)

```
 1  Tim:    Is it all frozen?=
 2  Mary:   =No. this part of it's fine. Okay, when you pee::l it,
 3  Ben:    °Uh huh°
 4  Mary:   sli:ce it in fou:r.=lengthways (a n d t h e n)
 5  Ben:                         (Oh and then jus)
 6  Mary:   just take the seeds out=
 7  Tim:    =Or alternatively slice it in ha::lf, and use a teaspoon,
 8          ((banging sound)) and run it along.
 9          (0.3)
10  Mary:   You can choose whichever method you, pre:fer.=
11  Tim:    =(And) obviously there is gonna be politics (.)
12          (depending on which method you choose)=
13  Mary:   (>h u h< h e h  h e h  h e: h ) =Absolutely.
14          ((rustling sound))
15          (0.4)
16  Mary:   No there won't.=
17          =((banging sound))
18          (0.8)
19          ((rustling sound))=
20  Ben:    =Secretly there will be though
21          (0.4)
22  Mary:   Heh?
23  Ben:    SECRETLY THERE WILL BE=
24          =ehh °heh heh heh°
```

So, on the one hand, we have an imaginary analyst who *assumes* – given their general knowledge and experience of specific issues and topics – that certain work, say power relations emerging through the institutions or structures of gender and family, are *obviously* going on in this encounter. On the other hand, we have an imaginary analyst who will and can ignore all their assumptions and will only ever talk about the work of gender or family in this encounter when it is *orientated to* and *shown to be orientated to by the participants themselves.*

The problem that this debate eludes ties into this observation: is the 'fact' that Ben is Mary's son, 16, a teenager, a schoolboy, an 'A'-level student, white, male, able-bodied, British, or any other identities relevant to the interaction? Similarly, which of Mary's multiple identities are relevant: her age, her educational level, her gender, her job, her identity as mother of Ben, her identity as friend of Tim? Or is it that, at certain moments in this encounter, specific identities and related social structures emerge as relevant for the participants at specific moments in the encounter?

For example, Ben is faced with two possible ways to prepare this cucumber. And Mary says to him 'You can <u>ch</u>oose whichever method you, pre:<u>fer</u>' (10), which offers a potential way out for Ben, he does not have to follow her instructions (or Tim's). Tim then comments that '=(And) obviously there is gonna be politics (.) [depending on which method you choose]=' (11–12). A question to ask is, what is the 'politics' that Tim is referring to? Is this tied to the institution of family, that Ben, *as Mary's son*, is faced with – if he follows Tim's instructions he is therefore rejecting his mother's advice? Or is it tied to another institution, say the institution of friendship?

We have nothing in the video to specifically say that, at that moment, this is about the paired identities of parent and teenager. None of the participants *explicitly* orientate to the social institution of family and the rights and responsibilities that belonging to this category produce. The talk that follows Tim's comment does not show them, or us – the overhearing audience – what specifically he is referring to. Mary laughs, then agrees with quite a humorous tone in her voice, then repeals that agreement and says slightly more seriously 'No there won't' (16) as she gets up to leave the table. Ben then, again with a humorous tone, disagrees with her statement, Mary does not hear this and so Ben repeats his comment and she laughs. They all just seem to get the joke.

So what can we actually say about Tim's use of the word 'politics'? One option is to say that Tim is referring to the dilemma that *anyone* is faced with when having to choose between two sets of opposing instructions and that family and/or friendship does not really come into it. And we could go and look for other examples where people are faced with a similar dilemma and see how the participants orientate to it. But this does not reduce my feeling – or maybe I should say my assumption – that this is, *at least in part*, tied to Ben's position as Mary's son, that the 'politics' that Tim refers to is tied, at least in part, to the interpersonal politics of family and friendship. We could search through the rest of this encounter and other encounters between these people and look at other similar moments, to see when and how Mary and Ben's relationship as parent and teenager or mother and teenager is explicitly a topic of the talk. This may give us some clues. We could also speak to the participants and ask them about the encounter. Well, I was one of the people and I can't really remember why that specific word.

So as Ben is faced with a dilemma, so are we as analysts: which version to go with – only, very closely, sticking to just what the participants orientate to at just that moment, or going with our hunches or trying to collect other moments where similar work occurs? And looking at recordings of other encounters, alongside my knowledge of those other encounters, alongside my knowledge of being a sur-rogate parent to another teenager, does help me, as the dilemma of 'whose advice to follow' often occurs and is sometimes explicitly talked about in connection with the politics of parenting. But this is my analytic solution; others will disagree and argue that I am making far too many assumptions and straying away from only relying on what the participants themselves are doing at just that moment.

My discussion of Extract 1 also raises other, related, debates. These include:

- The hidden role of the analyst's knowledge when making claims.
- The focus on very brief extracts of action and interaction.
- The focus on naturally occurring data and local contexts.
- The absence of any discussion about power.

I now want to briefly explore each of these points.

The hidden role of the analyst

Arminen (2000) gives us the following example from someone talking in an Alcoholics Anonymous (AA) meeting. At one point someone, let us call him Jim, says:

Extract 2 (Arminen, 2000, p. 43)

Jim: in a way this pe:rson kept me sober cause
        he just couldn't- (1.0) didn't want to drink
        himself

Now Jim *could* have said something like this:
    'In a way this person kept me sober cause he just **couldn't** drink himself'
    But instead, he ends up saying this:
    'In a way this person kept me sober cause he just **didn't want to** drink himself'
    And what Jim did was repair his talk; rather than saying that this other person was '**unable** to drink', instead he pauses and then describes this person as '**unwilling** to drink'. So Jim's self-repair gives a very specific identity to the person being spoken about. And Jim is giving this person an AA identity – that

this person is someone who every day volunteers not to drink. As Arminen notes, *without specific knowledge about AA's 'voluntary' ethos* – that an alcoholic is always an alcoholic and has to decide every day that they do not want to drink – the significance of Jim's self-repair may remain unnoticed.

So, to get a sense of the work that Jim is doing, you as an analyst need some insiders' or members' knowledge. To understand what Jim is orientating to, to fully adopt a stance of where you *only* focus on what the participants themselves are actually doing and attending to and not making any analytic assumptions, 'may depend on *an analyst's ability to recognize* the participants' situated competencies that have informed their activities' [my emphasis] (Arminen, 2000, p. 44). The ability to hear or see that a particular gesture or action is doing particular work depends, in part, on your ability to recognize just why they were doing what they were doing at that point.

Importantly, Arminen (2000) is not arguing that adopting the participants' orientation is a rhetorical trope, rather he shows us some of the *possible* problematics of this position. For me, how I come to understand certain moments of interaction can *at some moments* depend on my ability, as a culturally competent member of a specific community. I became very aware of this, at its most fundamental level, at three moments. Two of these moments highlighted my position as a native English speaker and the taken-for-granted knowledge that this provides:

- On one occasion I was in a data session with someone working with transcripts that were based on a Finnish-to-English translation. We kept exploring various paths that the transcript appeared to make relevant, only to be told that 'actually, in Finnish, the inferences aren't really like that'.
- Similarly, whilst in Finland, in a data session working with audiotapes of my data and other discussions, I became aware that I had to translate and explain some of the specific terminology, phrases and patterns of speech that the participant used.

Another occasion nicely showed me that to understand what is going on you sometimes need to actually see things from the participants' perspective:

- I kept noticing that as my next-door neighbours left their house they kept looking at and in my car. At first I thought that this was tied to their 'admiration' of my shiny new car or maybe they where checking what was in the car. Over time, I kept noticing them look at and in my car and thought that they must *really* like it. One day, I was standing by my car and I finally got a sense of what I am certain was actually going on: they were using the reflective quality of the windows as a surrogate mirror to 'check their appearance' just prior to going out. From then on, whenever I saw them look at my car I also focused more on the actions that then followed this and this confirmed my hunch, as after looking they would often re-style their hair or re-align items of clothing.

This position, *acknowledging the role of your own knowledge in making sense of what is going on for participants*, does not in any way deny that attending to participants' orientations *is the central task of analysis*. It does highlight some of the possible problematics you could encounter when your research is in contexts where specialist or technical talk or routines are practised. In such cases, you need to gain a certain level of members' knowledge or, as Lynch (1993) calls it, 'vulgar competence', of the language and routines of your research site.

Just focusing on brief moments of interaction

As you should realize by now, given the above discussions, a central feature of this type of work is that your key proof for your analytic claims is what participants are actually doing and saying. So your claim that someone is 'asking a question' is actually proved by someone else then 'giving an answer', or in some cases when an answer is not given, by the question-asker saying 'Hey I asked you a question' or re-asking the question and then getting an answer. This is sometimes called the 'next-turn proof procedure', in that when you are trying to get a sense about what a specific stretch of talk or action is doing, you can look at:

- the talk or actions of other participants just beforehand, the prior-turns, to see that what this person's talk or action is a response to and therefore what they are trying to do;
- the talk or actions of other participants just after it, the next-turns, to see how others understood and reacted to it and therefore what they understood it to be doing.

This can obviously be a very powerful way to make claims about your materials, especially when you provide your readers with transcripts of the encounters so they can also see and check (and argue with) your analysis.

However, interactions do not always occur as 'one-off' encounters, they are often just one in an ongoing series of encounters. Equally, topics or things raised at one moment may not get resolved at just that moment, they may be returned to much later in the same encounter or in other later encounters. I have a nice, albeit quite extreme, example of the serial nature of conversation and meaning. I met a friend, John, in the street and we then had a five-minute conversation about the stress in his life at that moment and how he was dealing with it. A few days later I met up with his girlfriend and she asked me 'How did you know I was getting married to John?' John had understood our conversation about 'stress' to refer to them planning their wedding and that his girlfriend had already told me about this. She was surprised by this, as she was definite that she had not told me. For me, the conversation about 'John's stress' was tied to him leaving one job and starting another as well as buying a new house. What I love about this is that for John and myself, the conversation made sense, or rather we both made sense of the topic 'John's stressful life' in two different ways. And our conversation went smoothly, we did not engage in any repair work at that moment, the question of meaning only emerged as an issue some days later. The point of this story is not that you should only focus on a series of encounters but that you should be aware of *the temporal and evolving nature of talk, actions and meanings in encounters* – and this occurs within a single encounter and over series of encounters.

Working with the local contexts of focus group and interview data

Firth and Kitzinger (1998) explore the contrasting ways that self-report data can be, and is, analyzed. They use focus group data, gathered around the topic of 'Women Saying "No" to Sex', to argue for talk from interviews and focus groups to be analyzed in respect of the local context of its production. They offer two readings of the same data taken from focus groups with women on the topic of saying 'no' to sex.

In the focus groups the women routinely talked about the emotional implications of refusing sex, especially 'hurting men's feelings'. Such self-reports are often referred to as 'emotion work' and used as a way to know about the behaviour and psychologies of the women *beyond the space of the focus group*. By adopting 'emotion work' as an *analysts' category*, such data is used to argue that women

> are engaged in emotion work as a routine part of sexual negotiation ... they are subjugating their own feelings (of disinterest in or distaste for sex) to those of their male partners (by engaging in sex when *he* wants to), or they are punishing themselves for prioritizing their own feelings (i.e., by refusing to have sex but then feeling guilty). (authors' emphasis) (Firth and Kitzinger, 1998, p. 310)

In this way the concept of 'emotion work' is used by the analyst to show what women *experience* when refusing sex. Such an analysis is silent on the local context of these womens' descriptions – that these descriptions are emerging in interaction with others in the focus group.

Firth and Kitzinger then use the concept of 'emotion work' as a *participants' category* and show a sensitivity to how 'talking about emotions when discussing sexual refusal' produces you as a specific type of person. They show how such talk about emotions constructs the men whom they describe refusing sex with as 'emotionally vulnerable, full of self-doubt' (1998, p. 311). By doing such talk about emotions, the women in the focus group both construct themselves as emotionally strong (as the men are emotionally weak and in need of support) and hence *not* victims, whilst reflexively producing women as responsible for the 'emotional work' in relationships. As they note:

> The reasons why women do – or *say* they do – 'emotion work' may be located not in women's psychologies (their need for approval, their 'naturally' caring natures, or adherence to the feminine sex-role stereotype) but in the social world they inhabit. ... (W)e mean this not simply in the sense that a heteropatriarchal world might harness and exploit women's allegedly greater emotional fluency, but in the sense that talk about doing 'emotion work' may offer women a legitimate and socially acceptable language for explaining and justifying their actions, and for presenting themselves (to themselves and others) in a favourable light. (authors' emphasis) (1998, p. 316)

Their work highlights that *an analysis of interview data or focus group data should be sensitive to how the talk is produced*. As they note:

> Extracts from talk are (often) assumed to 'speak for themselves'. But ... data extracts are (often) decontextualised and interpreted as if they were produced in a neutral and disinterested way by research participants anxious only to report on their lives as accurately and faithfully as possible. This leaves out the crucial fact that talk is always occasioned and produced in a context, in interaction with others – and that participants are orientating towards the questions, concerns, assumptions, interpretations and judgements of others in producing their talk. When social scientists make the methodological leap from what people 'say' to what they 'believe' or how they 'behave' they obscure the *social* function of talk and obscure its role *as talk-in-interaction*. (authors' emphasis) (1998, p. 317)

Working with power (and other key concepts)

The critique is often extended that by only focusing on the local context you can routinely miss the broader, 'underlying', structures and institutions. As I have tried to outline, especially in the last chapter on documents-in-use, this critique can misread the point of this style of work. It is not arguing that power or asymmetry is somehow absent from the encounters that it studies, but rather it wants to re-specify the way we engage and work with these and other overarching concepts.

Many concepts that are the day-to-day stock in trade of social, psychological and cultural analysis – like inequality, gender, cognition, attitude, law or bioscience – are often used quite uncritically by those analysts. For example, to talk of 'medicine' loses the multiplicity of fields, divisions and branches of 'medicine', and within these medicine*s* there are multiple numbers of competing and complementary histories, theories and practices about how to work on, know and understand such things as 'patients'. And this does not include thinking about how the academy, the state, law, business, charities, families, et cetera, are mutually entangled in various aspects of 'medicine'. Relatedly, if you could get funding (and ethical approval) for a team of researchers to actually follow 'an individual patient' as they enter a hospital, say onto a ward, you could follow them as an embodied subject, follow various blood and urine samples, follow various medical records, charts, results and scans, follow the various electronic and paper-based documents that flow between spaces (including kitchens, research and accounts departments), follow the various conversations that happen about just that patient within the ward, at people's homes, and so on.

This style of work does not always just accept the taken-for-granted ways that we understand, talk about and undertake our work. In so doing it often makes the broad themes and concepts of social, psychological and cultural analysis a lot messier than they first appear. As my favourite maxim puts it: *We think in generalities but we live in detail.* As such, a focus on the local context does not ignore the broader themes and concepts, rather it often asks you to think differently about them and so, maybe, you will begin to ask different questions. I am just going to offer a very brief example that engages with the issues of power and authority in a specific medical context.

In recent years we have seen a rise in calls for 'patient-centred medicine' and the end to 'medical paternalism'. We should no longer just silently follow our doctor's advice but rather we should be encouraged to ask questions, have our concerns listened to and have our views taken into account. With this new-found voice, patients then become 'empowered'. I want to focus on a medical consultation that according to this theory represents very bad practice – where the voice of the patient is silenced. This is taken from a first meeting between a mother and a doctor from a paediatric cardiology unit and they are discussing what action to take next about her child.

Extract 3 (Silverman, 1987, p. 80 – slightly modified transcript)

Doctor: Well it seems to me that her catheter needs to be repeated. (   ) Well really she's in a bit of heart failure actually. Her liver's quite big, heart's big, you know, she's really (   ) small, she's not growing up OK. (   )

Doctor: So what we'll do is to review the film. It looks as if she should have something done. We don't want to risk any damage being done to her lungs(really

Mother: (No no.

Doctor: It's a rather complex situation though. It's not easy to decide what to do. She's a little bit blue really isn't she? (If we

Mother: (On and off

Doctor: On and off. And if we (0.5) try and put a band on her pulmonary artery, its effect will be to make her more blue

Mother: Mmmm.

Doctor: Anyway (1.0) We'll have a talk and see what we think is the best thing to do

Mother: Mm.

Doctor: And I'll write to you. But I think she'll have to have a catheter test.

Note how, in this example, the mother is simply told what is going to happen next with her child. Even when she works to resists the doctor's comment 'She's a little bit blue really isn't she?', by saying 'On and off', the doctor simply repeats what she has said and continues to tell what they are going to do. Compare this style of consultation to another mother's encounter, within the same clinic.

Extract 4 (Silverman, 1987, pp. 142–5 – slightly modified transcript)

Doctor: Well how is she? Dr X has written to me and has also sent the catheter films that were done in Othertown. Um, can I ask you a few questions? How is she in her self?

Mother: Well, I've been pleasantly surprised to be quite honest. ((She goes onto relate details of cold, chest infections and episodes of breathlessness))

Doctor: Do you think her breathlessness interferes with her enjoying doing things or not?

Mother: Well, not, not at the present.
  ...

Doctor: We know from the, er, catheter that Dr. X sent us that she has a complicated heart abnormality. It's the sort of abnormality that is always difficult to correct. ((Dr. continues by reviewing the risks of surgery at length))

Doctor: That could be counter-balanced with: what is her life going to be without the operation? The answer is to that is, probably very good. She may well have a relatively normal childhood.

Mother: Yes.
  ...

Doctor: (The handicap will be) perhaps not enough to interfere with her pleasure in play and walking and doing things

In this consultation the mother is asked a series of questions about what she actually thinks about her child and her condition. Also, note how the child is not discussed purely as a set of *symptoms* and *clinical conditions* but rather as a someone, *a social being*.

According to the theories of patient-centredness and empowerment, the second encounter is an example of good practice. The mother's point of view is taken into account, the child is discussed as a person rather than as an object in need of technical repair work. With the first example, in contrast, the diagnosis is delivered in a very blunt way, without any discussion about what the parent might want. So we have two different consultation styles, and Silverman notes that one produces the child as a 'clinical object' and the other as a 'social object'. What is interesting to discover is that the second version – where the doctor would allow parents to make the choice about what to do next and encourage the parents to focus on non-clinical matters like the child's enjoyment of life or friendly personality – was *atypical*. This consultation style would *only* be used if the child had an additional handicap of Down's syndrome, as well as suspected cardiac disease. In these cases, the doctors would focus on the non-medical world of 'happy children at play' and encourage parents to talk about this. And this style of consultation – an 'empowering' and 'patient-centred consultation' – was used to *dissuade parents* from further medical intervention. And Silverman (1987) clearly shows – demonstrating one of Michel Foucault's famous observations – how power can work as much by encouraging persons to speak, as by silencing them.

Some closing comments

For me, academics (among many others) spend a lot of time, energy and words on arguing that someone else's approach is 'nearly right but, then again, absolutely wrong'. There are no hard-and-fast answers or solutions to any of the debates and dilemmas you will face when undertaking work on conversations and texts. It often depends on what you read, how you read it, and what just makes sense to you in the context of your own work. Above all, I would suggest going and reading examples of as many people's empirical work as you have time for, to get a sense about the practical decisions they made and the practical solutions they employed.

I want to leave the final word on the topic of the debates and dilemmas I have engaged with to someone I like reading, Harvey Sacks (and note that we could equally exchange the words 'talk' and 'conversation' for 'texts' and 'discourse'):

So, the work I'm doing is about talk. It's about the details of talk. In some sense it's about how conversation works. The work tends to change, and let me just say a little about what I plan to do here. I have a bunch of stuff and I want to see whether an order for it exists. Not that I want to try to order it, *but I want to try to see whether there's some order to it.* (my emphasis) (1995, Fall 67, p. 622)

≡≡≡ **Key points**

- Acknowledging the role of your own knowledge in making sense of what is going on in your data does not in any way deny that attending to what participants are actually doing or talking about is the central task of analysis.
- A focus on the local context of an interaction does not ignore the broader themes and concepts like power or inequality, rather it often asks you to think differently about them and so, maybe, you will begin to ask different questions.

Further reading

The topics of this chapter are considered in more detail in the following works:

Billig, M. (1999) 'Whose terms? Whose ordinariness? Rhetoric and ideology in conversation analysis', *Discourse and Society*, 10(4): 543–58.
Schegloff, M. (1997) 'Whose text? Whose context?', *Discourse and Society* 8: 165–87.
Wetherell, M. (1998) 'Positioning and interpretative repertoires: conversation analysis and post-structuralism in dialogue', *Discourse and Society*, 9: 387–412.

9
Exploring documents

Chapter objectives
After reading this chapter, you should

- see various ways that you can engage with documents and texts;
- know more about 'orphaned texts', 'texts-in-abstract', or 'texts-as-things-in-themselves', where the social life of the text itself is the object of your analysis;
- see some potential ways to engage with texts, to try to offer you access to a range of questions and tactics you might want to adopt when engaging with texts; and
- be aware of an 'analytic attitude' that might help you make sense of how texts are organized, how texts speak to us, and how you can begin to interrogate them in order to understand the organization of contemporary institutions.

Thinking about what is there (and not there)

Exploring a text often depends as much on *focusing on what is said* – and how a specific argument, idea or concept is developed – as well as *focusing on what is not said* – the silences, gaps or omissions. To explore what I mean, look at the following dating advertisement I found in my local free newspaper:

- **ATTRACTIVE LADY**, medium-build, 5ft 5" very caring, considerate, GSOH, seeks gentleman for friendship/ltr, must be potty about animals, like eating out and going out socially for a quiet drink.
  (Source: *Newcastle Herald and Post*, 2004)

For a start, one thing that is noticeably absent is any specific reference to this woman's age. We have no clues about her age – say terms like 'young' or a numerical category like '32'. Also, we have no clues as to the age of the person she would like to meet – say 'seeking man 35–45' or '40+' – which could offer us clues as readers as to which age she might belong.

So 'age' is a silence in this text. Obviously, other things are silent and we actually have an unlimited number of things that are 'not there'; we have no discussion of her shoe size, whether she visits her doctor regularly or whether she has ever dreamed of winning an Olympic medal. The point is that, given the immediate context and our cultural knowledge about dating, the omission of her age is, potentially, *a noticeably absent feature of the text*. If you read through the other dating advertisements in this paper, the massive majority – 121 – have some reference to their own age or the age of the person they would like to meet. Only 11 ads are without any specific reference to age. With most papers, when we read such ads, we just expect an age to be there so that we can judge whether we might want to reply. And this ties into our culturally shared knowledge and expectations that we routinely seek to date people roughly within our age group.

So do we have any other clues to understanding what her age is? Well, the context may help us: if this ad was in a newspaper or magazine specifically targeted at a specific age group – say a publication aimed at over 60s or 20-somethings – we may reflexively understand that this person is either from that target age group or would like to meet someone within that age group. In this case, the paper is a local, free, newspaper, and the other ads cover all age ranges. Another clue might be to focus on what descriptions she actually chooses. Note how she describes herself as a 'lady' and that she 'seeks gentleman'. The categories lady and gentleman belong together and produce a slightly more specific reading of her age as 'lady' and 'gentleman' are unlikely to be understood, in this context, as teenagers, or in their twenties or thirties. Also, this is not a 'young lady' or a 'mature lady' or any other version, and she is not seeking a 'toy-boy' or just 'a man'. So we can get a sense – given our cultural competence – that this lady *could be*, say, over 40, given that a lady and a gentleman are often tied to certain behaviours and activities like 'being civilized', 'having good manners' or 'enjoying culture'. Such descriptions are not the currency of contemporary youth culture, although that is not say that such descriptors, behaviours or activities are not available to people of all ages.

We can take this reading further, if we focus on *how the different elements of the text combine to further consolidate (or disrupt) the meaning*. For example, this is not only a lady seeking a gentleman but a lady that 'seeks a gentleman for friendship/ltr'. So, she is not seeking 'a gentleman for wild passionate nights' or seeking 'a hunky gentleman for fun and frolics'. The elements of such descriptions are potentially at odds with each other: does gentleman routinely fit with 'wild passion' or does gentleman fit with 'hunky'? What she seeks is 'friendship' and 'ltr' – which I take to mean, given the context that this is a dating ad, long-term relationship. And 'friendship', 'long-term relationship', 'gentleman' and 'lady' all fit together to produce some notion of 'being civilized'. Note also that she describes herself as 'very caring, considerate', which again ties and reflexively consolidates this reading. Note also that the gentleman must like 'going out socially for a quiet drink.' – the potential couple are unlikely to be going clubbing or engaging in all-night drinking sessions. We hear 'quiet drink' as drinking alcohol, not tea or coffee, in moderation, in a 'civilized' way.

I could continue to explore just this dating ad in this way. I could continue to study all the 132 ads in just this paper, and say something about how the institution of 'age' is a feature of all the ads and the work 'age' does. I would definitely focus on all those ads where age is not explicitly described and try to make sense of both how age is implicit (or not) in those ads and the work achieved when age is *not* a mentionable alongside focusing on the range of work that mentioning age does in the other ads. I could also look at other dating ads, say in more age-targeted or leisure or lifestyle-specific publications, and see the role it performs there. Hopefully, you can see how my analysis is made possible by both reading *with* and *against* the grain of the text and focusing on how the different elements work together.

Arguing the case

When studying texts you are also interested in *the rhetorical work of the text*, how the specific issues it raises are structured and organized and chiefly *how it seeks to persuade you* about the authority of its understanding of the issue. Below, I have given you a brief extract from a newspaper article with the title 'New wave of "sophisticated" alcopops fuels teenage binge drinking':

> Teenagers are gripped by an 'epidemic' of binge-drinking so severe it has seen consumption almost double in the past decade, health experts are warning as the nation begins its Christmas celebrations in earnest.
>
> Figures released last week reveal the average alcohol consumption of children aged 11 to 15 has rocketed from 5.3 units a week in 1990 to 9.8 a week last year. Of the 86% of 15-year-olds who drink, boys consume an average of 13.8 units – the equivalent of seven pints of beer or lager – and girls, 10.7 units. This consumption is crammed into one or two nights' drinking.
>
> 'What we're seeing is an epidemic of binge-drinking,' says Andrew McNeill, of the Institute for Alcohol Studies (IAS). 'By the time you're 15, getting slaughtered is a central part of your social activities.' The new research, gleaned by the Department of Health through surveys in 285

schools, pinpoints the likely cause: alcopops, or flavoured alcoholic beverages (FABs).

While the number of teenagers who drink has not risen dramatically – with 26% of 11- to 15-year-olds having drunk in the past week compared to 21% in 1999 – the popularity of such drinks has escalated. About 68% of pupils who had drunk in the past week drank alcopops in contrast to just 37% three years earlier. The rise puts the drinks on a par with cider, beer and lager.

Perhaps most worryingly, 77% of teenage girl drinkers opt for them. 'The introduction of alcopops does not seem to have affected the number of pupils who drink but it has contributed to the increase in the total amount drunk,' adds the report. (Source: Hall, 2002, *The Guardian*)

Note, first of all, *the range of sources of knowledge and evidence* the article draws on: we have health experts' warnings, we have the Department of Health and someone from the Institute for Alcohol Studies. In this way, it appears that at least three different authoritative sources of knowledge have been drawn on. However, it is unclear as to whether the Department of Health's report was produced by the Institute for Alcohol Studies or who quite makes up the group of health experts. Later in the article, we have other sources including:

- Academy – a professor of liver medicine and a professor of cardiology.
- Brewery industry – a spokeswoman, a managing director and an untitled other.
- Charities – the chief executive of Alcohol Concern, head of policy of the Portman Group.
- Politics – a former Health Secretary.

In this way, a range of 'interested' and 'disinterested' parties are used to explore and outline the potential areas of the debate. The text appears more balanced and the journalist, the paper (and journalism as a whole) mere 'neutral' observers and describers of the debate. Note how other, potentially relevant voices – like the family, the police, the Church – are not drawn on. The teenagers are spoken for and about by specific, more knowledgeable, others.

Also, note just how we come to know about these teenage drinkers, *the forms and modes of knowledge and evidence* that are employed. We are not simply told that there is a binge-drinking problem for teenagers, but rather we are *shown* the configuration of the problem. We are given a range of statistics and figures about alcohol units (alongside a translation into the language of pints), as well as verbatim quotes from an expert and a verbatim quote from the Department of Health report. And note how some of the expertise is rendered; it is not just someone from the 'Institute for Alcohol Studies (IAS)', or a spokesperson, but rather '**Andrew McNeill**, of the Institute for Alcohol Studies (IAS)' and it is his claim and just his claim that there is an **'epidemic** of binge-drinking'. The term '"epidemic"', when first used, is used in quotation marks, so as to distance the paper from being the author of this claim. Also, the research is not simply based on 'surveys in … schools' but rather more precisely 'surveys in **285** schools'. So among other things we have the power of numbers, the science of statistics and the voice of (trusted and independent) experts informing us just what is going on.

Expanding an argument

Unsurprisingly, I could continue to explore the newspaper article in a multitude of ways. I could focus on how this and other newspaper articles work to be 'neutral' and 'unbiased' to offer all sides of the debate – how it works to just present the 'facts of the case'. In so doing I might also want to focus on the moments when this veil of neutrality seems to more visibly slip, for example when the increase in alcohol consumption is described as having 'rocketed' over say using terms like 'risen' or 'grown'. And it is not hard to see – and in part this book is concerned with exactly this point – that descriptions are never neutral but produce a specific version or understanding of the world.

I might instead focus on how the identities or subject positions of 'teenage binge drinker' or 'binge drinker' are produced, over different texts, as a problem, a figure of concern, action and debate. In the newspaper article above, we can see the problem as tied to a configuration of health, age and gender. Note especially the last paragraph where teenage girls are rendered as a (or maybe *the*) new figure of concern. So a question to ask is: *how are specific identities produced, sustained or negotiated within texts?*

In another article I found, we have the same configuration explored, albeit in relation to 'young women'. The heading for the article reads: 'Binge drinking: do they mean us?' The article offers a quote from a young woman:

> Molly, a 21-year-old student, is shocked at the suggestion that she is a binge drinker: 'Having three glasses of wine in a night more than about four or five times a month counts as binge drinking? That is not binge drinking. That's called having a social life. A little alcohol lightens you up. Obviously there are those who take it too far, and they should be specifically targeted rather than heaping stigmas on normal girls who just want to have a laugh – like their male counterparts'. (Source: Asthana and Doward, 2003, *The Observer*)

In contrast to the one above, this article seeks evidence from those categorized as 'binge drinkers' and raises questions about the configuration of this new subject position. Molly's story documents some re-occurring features of the discourse of binge drinking, including:

- Debates about what amount should be understood as 'normal drinking', 'having a laugh' or as 'a problem'.
- Debates about alcohol being good for you and only a 'real' problem for a minority.
- Debates about how women are being stigmatized for doing what men have always done.

I could extend the analysis to focus on the issue of how young women and alcohol is part of the broader debate about the position of women in society. The discourses about women and binge drinking often rely on, either explicitly or implicitly, the assumption that alcohol produces a more predatory, sexualized and 'unfeminine' femininity alongside the fear of men taking advantage of drunken women and the moral decline in public life. Does this, in part, trade on the discourse that women should not be sexually active or independent?

Finally, we could explore these articles', and others' texts, to discover some of the assumptions that configure binge drinking as 'a problem'. We could ask: Is this a medical problem? A public health problem? A public order problem? A hybrid of all these and more? How activities or groups of people are configured as 'a problem' and who names and describes the problem will define the range of potential solutions that can and will be offered. With this in mind, I want to outline how I worked with some academic texts that discuss and understand 'the problem' of how to encourage general practitioners (GPs) to give alcohol-related advice.

Whose problem, whose solution?

As part of a project on how GPs talk about alcohol in consultations, I decided to look at the academic literature on the topic. Luckily, one of my colleagues has done a lot of research on trying to implement a specific form of alcohol intervention in primary care – something called brief interventions (BI). So in order to initially explore this topic, I just had to go into her room and search through her filing cabinet. I was faced with a mass of research papers on the topic of BI; over the past twenty years, through repeated rounds of funding from the World Health Organization, an academic industry has grown which seeks to develop, evaluate and implement BI. My solution to exploring her archive was to start by looking at all the articles written by authors whose surname began with 'A' and work through the texts one by one.

Every day I would go to the filing cabinet and pull out a few articles, photocopy and then sit down and read them, re-read them and make notes on the ones that were relevant. Initially I was just reading them to get a sense of how BI was talked about in these articles and the general directions of the debates and questions that the articles sought to engage with. I then tried to think about how all these articles related to each other – what were the overarching issues that kept getting returned to. I had probably got to about 'G' or 'H', say about thirty or forty articles in, when it struck me what was at stake in these texts. I then went through some of the other articles to explore and check this hunch.

The issue – one of the issues that fascinated me and seemed to offer some analytic mileage – is raised in a lot of the BI literature. I first noticed it as I realized that many of the papers I was reading had very similar introductory sections. Below is a very typical example of the opening section of a BI paper:

> Recent outcome evaluation studies have provided compelling evidence that brief intervention in primary health care settings will facilitate significant reductions in hazardous drinking. Despite this evidence most general practitioners either do not discuss drinking with their patients or only respond to obvious signs of major dependency. (Adams et al., 1997, p. 291)

Note the contrast that is set up in these statements: On the one hand there is 'evidence' that offering this style of intervention offers 'reductions' in problem drinking. On the other hand, GPs 'do not discuss drinking' or only work with a specific group of patients, those with extreme alcohol problems. And note that this is not just evidence but rather '**compelling** evidence' and this evidence does not just offer reductions but rather '**significant** reductions'.

The argument is that despite the evidence for BI, general practitioners are currently unwilling, or unable, to implement it. Also, these texts note that general practitioners are 'well placed' to implement BI and that the patients 'expect lifestyle advice'. In order to attend to this apparent mismatch between evidence and practice, these texts often focus on general practitioners' attitudes to, experiences of and management of alcohol and alcohol-related problems. The aim is that by doing such research with GPs the researchers can understand why they are not currently doing it and therefore find ways to encourage GPs to do it. Put simply, the *problem* in the texts is just this: we know this thing works, we show you that this thing works, but you are still not doing it. The *solution* is to try to understand why you are not doing it and then develop ways to persuade you to do it.

Importantly, we should ask *what are the assumptions in these texts?* And one of the assumptions in these texts is that the GPs would understand the evidence as 'compelling' or agree that these reductions are 'significant'. So you could ask questions like: Who is this evidence 'compelling' for and in whose terms are the reductions 'significant', GPs or this research community? Another assumption, if not *the* assumption, is that the problem is *the GPs*. But we could think about this differently, *to read these texts and these arguments sceptically, to misread them.* By misread, I mean not to simply accept the argument in the texts but rather to repeatedly argue with and question the trajectory of the arguments. For example, rather than understanding these texts to be concerned with such topics as 'The implementation of brief intervention in routine general practice' (Aalto **117** and Seppa, 2001, p. 431), it enables us to think through this trend as being concerned with an alternative trajectory, *the implementation of general practice in routine brief intervention.* The question to ask is *not* 'Why is it that general practitioners do not use BI?' but rather '*Why is it that BI wants to use general practitioners?*'

This then offers an alternative understanding and an alternative way to read and analyze these texts. The research questions I became interested in were connected to such questions as *why did they choose GPs to implement their programme of work?* I then went back to my archive to try to find an answer to this question. The earliest reference to 'why we should use GPs' is actually raised in terms of 'why we should use primary health care' – of which GPs are just one part. The argument for using primary health care was outlined as: 'The main reason for the choice is the need to start with a model which can be *translated relatively easily to a variety of settings and cultural groups*' [my emphasis] (Babor et al., 1986, p. 25). Here, the 'main reason' is not that primary health care can offer anything in particular, other than a *convenient context* for this programme of work that is transnational. In this sense, that primary health care is essentially a space of and for medical work, medical knowledge and medical expertise is, at best, secondary.

The text then goes on to outline the other benefits of employing this setting:

- It connects to issues that are important for those in this setting as alcohol problems are a significant source of mortality, morbidity and family problems.
- It offers a low-cost solution as it 'does not require a cadre of alcohol specialists but relies principally on the skills of individuals who are already in post and accessible to the population they serve' (Babor et al., 1986, p. 25).
- It enables easy replication of effective interventions as the settings are similar.

To be sure, the first point, that alcohol affects both the physical and social health of populations, is central to the aims of GPs and primary health care in general. However, the way that it offers a potential source of cheap and accessible labour and is a space the enables easily reproducible research does not immediately connect it to the medical expertise that such a setting offers. Unlike the prior discourses of the problem of alcohol – which emphasize that medicine *should* engage the problem in and through a 'disease model', that they *should* engage with the problem in and through their roles as 'medical experts' – the appeal for action has dramatically changed. Within the framework of BI, GPs are 'just well placed'.

As this example begins to demonstrate, hopefully you can see that it is worthwhile to sceptically engage with the assumptions embedded in texts. Also, it can be useful to trace the 'birth' and development of specific discourses and so offer alternative readings of the problem alongside alternative solutions.

Thinking about the history of our present

Some work with texts specifically focuses on how ideas, practices and identities emerge, transform, mutate and become the relatively stable things we have today. They seek to understand and describe the (historical) trajectory of the contemporary ideas, practices and identities we all currently just take for granted. Such 'histories of the present' remind us that what we take for granted often has complicated and esoteric beginnings. For example, May (1997) notes that

> At the beginning of the last century (the nineteenth), medicine and alcohol were drawn together to construct a new category of persons, which by the 1850s had acquired the label 'alcoholic' ... In Britain ... drunkenness ceased to be one of a number of normative states experienced by large sections of the population, and became a 'problem' that was opened up for reasoned dissection. (1997, pp. 170–1)

Habitual drunkenness is no longer to be understood simply as a 'sin' or a problem of social order. Habitual drunkenness is now routinely connected to both diseases of the body and diseases of the mind, most notably *addiction* and, in recent years, diseases of self-control, most notably *dependence*. It is now named as 'alcohol misuse', 'alcohol abuse', 'alcohol dependency' or 'alcoholism' and is opened up for 'reasoned dissection' by a range of experts in various scientific, medical and psychological disciplines. This style of work may lead to us to the question why exactly we act in just this way or why certain groups of people have the knowledge and power to understand and act on others. Importantly, it seeks to map the trajectories of these discourses, to outline the specific strategies that led to 'our present' as well as those that were rejected or seen to 'fail'.

Obviously, given its historical nature, this style of work often uses documents to explore specific topics or questions, although having said that, such 'histories' may focus on something that has emerged in the recent past, say, AIDS, and may also rely on other sources of materials. Also, rather than focus in great detail on a single text, these studies focus on a broad range of texts as they try to show the 'styles of thought' as they emerge, consolidate and compete across and between texts. For example, May's (1997) work on the historical emergence of and contemporary dilemma of alcohol addiction focuses on a range of texts, including an 1804 essay on drunkness, a 1917 book on shell shock, alongside more contemporary academic work on the history of addiction and psychological studies that seek to treat those who are addicted. Through this range of texts, May attempts to trace how the medicalization of addiction has only been partially successful; centrally he shows us how

> The construction of medical ideas about addiction have come to constitute the addict not simply as a social problem, but as a problem that

119

medicine itself finds difficult to understand ... The doctor may thus 'diagnose' an addictive state, but is powerless to effect recovery since this depends on the motivation and volition of the patient. (1997, p. 397)

Put simply, if the patient refuses the identity of 'addict', medicine is relatively powerless to act on that person. If the patient accepts the identity of 'addict', medicine is still relatively powerless, as they must rely on the patient's own self-motivation and can only really work to 'encourage' them. In order to explore how this style of work uses documents, I want to briefly offer you an example.

Case study: The discovery of doctors' 'minds' and 'bodies'

Gothill and Armstrong (1999) use texts to explore the history of general practitioners' present crisis of identity and purpose. The crisis in British general practice is often related to issues like increasing government regulation leading to a lack of professional autonomy and increasing patient demands that can lead to stress, mental health problems, substance abuse and suicide. The authors want to offer an alternative understanding of these contemporary dilemmas, one that focuses on and re-describes the taken-for-granted conceptions of the identity and role of general practitioners. They seek to offer 'an account of discursive practices in the construction of a human subject, a doctor' (1999, p. 2).

Initially, they focus on one text, Balint's article 'The doctor, his patient and the illness', which appeared in the medical journal, *The Lancet*, in 1955. The other texts that form their archive are articles and books that appear in what they call 'the general practice literature' from between 1955 and 1997. As they note:

There is of course a much larger literature on the doctor–patient relationship, much of it from the social sciences, but for the purposes of this paper, we shall restrict ourselves to texts recognised as belonging to the general practice literature rather than interpretations and perceptions of those outside the field. (1999, p. 11)

So their archive consists of a very bounded set of texts, both in relation to time and domain. I should note that such a strict demarcation of the arena of discourse is not that typical of such work but may reflect some of the pragmatic demands of the project they were working on.

They discover, trace and describe the formation of the doctor's subjectivity in and through these texts. They divide it into three main stages – inception, elaboration and control – which I have divided into three temporal periods:

The 1950s By focusing on Balint's (1955) 'seminal' paper, they show how the patient's 'mind', 'inner' or 'private life' became a legitimate object for doctors to examine. As Balint describes it, 'patients were not only willing to undergo, but demanded a psychological examination' (1955, p. 685). In this way, psychoanalytic techniques entered the consulting room and the patient's personal experience – all their behaviour – become potential sources of material for the doctor's expertise. Gothill and Armstrong comment that much of Balint's paper was

> concerned with the ethical dilemmas which arose in each encounter with an individual patient: deciding what should be seen and what left unseen; what should be said and left unsaid; what should be left organised and what left unorganised. (1999, p. 3)

Faced with these ethical dilemmas, the doctor became an 'individual-subject', rather than just a node of the impersonal, collective, medical gaze. One solution was the formation of 'Balint groups', where groups of doctors discussed – even examined – specific cases and sought to learn how to use these techniques to work sensitively and with intimacy. They must learn to avoid 'abusive interpretation' or 'cross-contamination between personal and professional relations' (1999, p. 4). The group facilitator's role was to focus these post-consultation examinations on the relationship *between* doctor and patient rather than overly exploring the doctors' or patients' 'inner life' and the group acted as an objective 'third person' in evaluating the behaviours of the consultation room. As Gothill and Armstrong argue:

> One might conclude that Balint's 'tactful and objective' third person had indeed been smuggled into the consultation room, concealed in the newly fractured identity of the professional self-conscious doctor. (1999, p. 5)

The 1960s and 1970s They then focus on a range of texts that extended Balint's argument, showing how various technologies emerged to understand, examine and name these new doctor/patient practices. This new relationship was named as shifting from 'illness-centred' to 'person-centred' medicine. One study audiotaped and transcribed doctor/patient consultations and described the styles and techniques of consultations as 'doctor-centred' and 'patient-centred'. Gothill and Armstrong note how

> terms which had previously defined the kinds of object defined by doctors (i.e. an illness or a patient) had mutated into descriptions of the point of view adopted by the examiner and, by implication, something about her character – her way of being as revealed in her way of seeing. (1999, p. 5)

One style of consultation focused on the language of exploring anatomy and physiology and the other on biography and psychology. Importantly, unlike more contemporary discussions, neither approach was seen as more or less 'empowering' for patients; it was, at that point, a question of preferred consultation style. However, those practising and advocating person/patient-centred styles were able to differentiate themselves from others and render themselves as more 'humane'. The doctor now had specific tools and techniques to explore the patient's 'inner world' but none to engage with their own.

The 1980s and 1990s   They then outline how their texts began to shift from a focus on the doctor/patient relationship to focus on 'the consultation' where specific consultation skills can be studied, learned and then performed. Students could learn these new skills through video-recording consultations, then discussing them with 'expert' others during feedback sessions. In this way, doctors could learn to be more 'effective'. As they explain it:

> The objective correlate of this process was a creation of an iconic representation of a prescribed style – an image of the doctor on the television screen which became not so much a means of learning, as an end in itself: the creation of a doctor, by a doctor, for view by other doctors. The doctor having acquired a voice in Byrne and Long's study, now developed a body, albeit a virtual image displayed on a screen; a communicating object strangely dissociated from a watching 'self' who was to observe, learn from and control it. (1999, p. 8)

They then shift the focus onto another text, which introduces and outlines to doctors the 'inner' or 'internal' conversations that they have when consulting with patients – the disrupting presence of doctors' 'confusing self-observation and criticism' (1999, p. 8). The doctors' body, each finger of their left hand, is also to be used to anchor specific 'checkpoints' to remind them to undertake key aspects of the consultation. Also the doctor's feelings are to be order; those unconstructive to the consultation – irrationality and selfishness – were to be excluded, while others – intuition and responsiveness – were to be included. So a new, self-aware and self-monitoring doctor appears where their thoughts and feelings are central to any definition or external evaluation of 'good' practice.

As you can see, this style of work is less centred on exploring, in intricate detail, the word-by-word or line-by-line production of discourse, but rather offers an overview of the central directions and shifts in the trajectory of a specific impulse. Their work outlines three interrelated ideas:

- That the disembodied clinical perception, which worked on depersonalized bodies, has been transformed, to include a focus on both the patients' and, increasingly, the doctors', personal, inner, experience.
- That a range of technologies, including 'confessional' groups, facilitators, audiotapes, verbatim transcripts, video cameras, video players and communication experts, have been central to these transformations.

- That it is not external power and control – from government or demanding patients – that has shifted identities and relations and is therefore key to this crisis, but rather how individual patients and doctors constantly regulate and monitor the minutiae of their own conduct, their 'self', and the conduct of others.

In presenting this history of our present, they work quite closely with some of the writings of the French philosopher Michel Foucault. And one of Foucault's interests was in how specific discourses, specific formations of what he called power/knowledge (in this case medical and psychological discourses), produce, shape and enable specific subjects (in this example general practitioners). It is not hard to think of the mass of subjectivities that could be investigated in this way, be it 'ethical consumers', 'diabetics' or 'homeless people', and the possible sources of texts you could draw on to understand how these people are 'made'.

Some closing comments

In this brief tour of working with document or texts, I cannot begin to do justice to the massive range of potential sources of material or the potential analytic trajectories that you can engage with. It is clear, given the vast number of texts that we engage with on a day-to-day basis – that seek to enrol us into a specific way of knowing, acting, being in and understanding the world – that taking the work of texts seriously is central to all thinking about the contemporary institutions of social life. Whether you spend all your time working with just texts, or they are just part of your archive, the best advice I can offer is to read them and then re-read, and above all engage with them 'sceptically'.

Key points

- Exploring a text often depends as much on focusing on what is said – and how a specific argument, idea or concept is developed – as well as focusing on what is not said – the silences, gaps or omissions. You can focus on how the different elements of the text combine to consolidate (or disrupt) meanings alongside the assumptions in the text.
- When studying a text you are also interested in how the specific issues it raises are structured and organized and how it seeks to persuade you about the authority of its understanding of the issue. You might want to focus on the range of sources of knowledge and evidence, alongside the forms and modes of the knowledge and evidence that are employed.

123

- You are often trying to document the specific discourses it draws on (and excludes) alongside the specific identities, or subject positions, that are produced, sustained or negotiated.

Further reading

Such a use of documents is outlined further by these authors:

Edley, N. (2001) 'Analysing masculinity: interpretative repertoires, ideological dilemmas and subject positions', in M. Wetherell, S. Taylor and S.J. Yates (eds), *Discourse as Data: A Guide to Analysis.* London: Sage, in association with The Open University, pp. 189–228.

Potter, J. (1996b) *Representing Reality: Discourse, Rhetoric and Social Construction.* London: Sage.

Wetherell, M., Taylor S. and Yates S.J. (eds) (2001) *Discourse Theory and Practice: A Reader.* London: Sage, in association with The Open University.

10
Studying discourse: some closing comments

Chapter objectives
After reading this chapter, you should

- have a broad overview on how to code and analyze all types of discursive materials;
- see how to draw together approaches to questioning the quality of analysis; and
- be aware of some main 'stepping-stones' when undertaking this style of work.

The aim of this book was to guide the reader in the planning, preparation and analysis of conversations, discourse and documents. Hopefully, you will now have a sense about some potential ways you could conduct a range of research projects. And at the end of this chapter I am going to offer you a 'checklist' of things you may want to consider as you undertake your own work. But first, I want to offer some general comments on the practicalities of coding, analyzing and writing up your work.

Coding, analyzing and thinking with your archive

Throughout this book, at various moments, I have offered comments about potential ways to code and analyze your archive of materials (see more details in

Gibbs, 2007). And on one level, the process of coding and analysis can seem quite 'routine'. You have your materials in front of you, you read and/or listen to/watch them, re-read and re-listen/watch them. You then note down some interesting themes or ideas or just something that strikes you as 'odd' or 'strange'. You may then start applying codes, key words or notes to various stretches of your texts to highlight specific, distinct, themes. You then re-read, applying the constant comparison method (Glaser, 1965) – where, for each new piece of 'data', you constantly make comparisons within and between your existing themes and so start to constantly refine your codes. Hopefully, you find a few negative instances or 'deviant cases' – moments in your material that just do not fit in with or contradict your prior understandings – that make you re-think and then refine your whole analysis (Seale, 1999). Your analysis develops until further collection of research materials yields no new themes for your analysis. Then you end up with a collection of extracts from texts or talk for each theme or code and a collection of ideas that you think are 'newsworthy' or important to tell others about. You have now generated some 'valid' and 'reliable' findings, so you write up what you have found (see more about this in Flick, 2007b).

Now that is one way to describe a process you often go through whilst doing analysis, or rather, it describes in rather practical terms what you sometimes practically do. However, the processes of coding, analyzing and checking your findings are always much messier than that. First and foremost, *analysis is always an ongoing process* that routinely starts prior to entering your research site, visiting that library or audiotaping that radio programme. As soon as I become interested in a specific topic, I will start to collect some literature on the topic, both 'academic' and 'non-academic'. This reading, alongside conversations with experts, past experiences and 'bizarre bolts from the blue' (often over a strong coffee), gives me some initial clues as to possible trajectories of the research, some research questions and analytic themes and codes. These diverse sources of knowledge often become analytic themes that I initially explore in my archive of materials. Other themes, ideas and topics routinely emerge in ad hoc and haphazard ways over the course of the research.

As I start to generate the archive, be it finding texts, recordings of 'naturally occurring' encounter or formal interviews, I will make notes on this process. These notes often cover both the 'successes' and the 'failures' of recruitment and the recording process alongside the gaps in the literature that may appear. All this provides me with more themes or questions to ask of my archive. In and through all this process, I am already making some 'analytic' choices about what is central to my research and what my research will focus on (and what will remain silent) – although more often than not, this is equally guided by constraints of time, money and the pragmatics of getting access to documents or people.

When I am in the field making notes, recording encounters or working with texts, I often try to see how the themes or ideas that I am currently thinking about compare to just what I am engaged with. In this sense, these very practical processes of research, constantly checking out your thoughts and hunches with each new piece of 'data', is a very informal and ad hoc version of the constant comparison method. Those incredibly memorable odd moments or extreme cases – what Emerson (2004) calls 'key incidents' – are also central, and also a practical version of 'deviant case analysis'. These are the moments where either you find that research article that argues a radically different case from all the others you have been reading, or that encounter you are recording seems to 'interactionally collapse' for all those taking part and may appear either as embarrassing, threatening or just funny. When you encounter these things, stretches of text or talk that make you re-think your prior understandings, you generally celebrate and go and recount your experience to others. These moments generally remain both memorable and storyable – they stay with you, you recount them in your formal and informal talks with both participants and colleagues, and they often appear as key findings when you write up your work.

When I am working with audio or video recordings, I initially just listen and/or watch the recordings once through as soon as I have time. I will make some notes and if any moments really stand out, I might even very roughly transcribe that section of talk. So again, my coding and analysis is both ongoing and refined and guided by what I feel is 'interesting' or 'noticeable'. When I have more time, I will then repeatedly listen/watch the tapes, and so generate, check and refine my analytic hunches. If I am working with a very small number of recordings or if I think a specific recording is vital, I might transcribe them all – to whatever level of detail I think is useful. With larger archives or recordings, I generally only transcribe those sections that are key – either because they are really good examples of what *typically goes on* or because they are *atypical* and therefore reflexively show what is routine. When I am undertaking work with interviews and/or focus groups I generally send my tapes to transcribers, which means I always have to check the transcript they produce against the tape and add any sort of detail that I am interested in (pauses, stress, overlapping speech). When it comes to sustained periods of analysis, I always prefer to re-listen to the tapes alongside re-reading the transcript. This allows me to get a sense (and re-remember) just what is it that was going on, rather than read a lot of 'flat' and interactionally docile transcripts.

I then try and write up the research (and re-write it, and re-write it) and in and through this process of writing more analysis occurs, as you further refine your ideas when you render them as text. Simultaneously, throughout the process described above, how I make sense of my archive is also directed by the journal article or book I have managed to find time to read. So hopefully you can see that analysis, in the sense of 'producing knowledge' about a specific body of materials, is an inherently ongoing accomplishment. And what is important to note is that this analytic process reflects both very theoretical and pragmatic concerns.

127

However, we still have to cover one final issue: why should anyone believe your thoughts about your materials?

Questions of quality and reflection

It is said that all qualitative researchers now face a 'double crisis':

- *A crisis of representation* – as the research text can no longer be assumed to 'capture' the lived experience or just present 'the facts' in the way once thought possible.
- *A crisis of legitimacy* – as the old criteria for evaluating 'the truthfulness' of accounts of qualitative research can no longer hold.

This crisis can be held in direct contrast to prior qualitative research, which (apparently) unambiguously valued and used words like 'validity' and 'reliability'. As Norman Denzin writes:

> Gone are the words like theory, hypothesis, concept, indicator, coding scheme, sampling, validity and reliability. In their place comes a new language: readerly texts, modes of discourse, cultural poetics, deconstruction. ... (1988, p. 432)

Denzin's list continues and he offers us access to the new language of research that some of you may already be conversant with.

To put it simply, *the crisis of legitimacy* is concerned with questioning two key 'positivist' notions about the quality of research: 'validity' and 'reliability'. These terms, and the approach they advocate, originally emerged out of a consensus vision about the possibility of scientific progress and argued that science could, and should, produce universal truth in and through the process of producing objective knowledge. So validity, from this perspective, 'refers to nothing less than truth, known through language referring to a stable social reality' (Seale, 1999, p. 34). And as you should understand by now, this whole book has been concerned with arguing against the very possibility of this view (see Flick, 2007b; Kvale, 2007).

In and through studying discourse you begin to see how there is not '*a* truth' but rather multiple and sometimes contradictory *truths or versions*. Also, language does not '*refer* to *a* stable reality' but *produces* multiple possible understandings of *the real*. However, this does not have to lead to a complete paralysis, that your work cannot say anything about what is going on in the texts or talk that you are studying. The point is to show, in and through your analysis and writing, how specific truths or versions of the world are produced. Your job is to convince others that *your claims, your interpretations*, are both *credible* and *plausible*, that you are not just making this up from thin air or this is just your vague hunch, but that *your argument is based on the materials from your archive*.

You have various practical solutions available to you to demonstrate to others that your argument is convincing and is based on the materials you collected:

- That you describe how you generated, worked with and analyzed your materials. You need to outline both the pragmatic and theoretical issues that directed this process.
- That you have checked and re-checked your ideas against your materials and searched for instances that might refute or contradict your claims. This will often be undertaken through some version of the constant comparison method and deviant case analysis.
- For your main or central analytic points you need to give your reader detailed access to the materials that led you to make those claims. For minor or subsidiary claims, you need to provide less evidence. You generally need to include sections or quotes from transcripts and/or texts.
- That you have checked your ideas against previous work by other authors on this topic. If your findings are radically different from prior work, you need to offer more materials to uphold your findings.
- That you have, if at all possible, presented or discussed your findings with those you have studied. Does your description make sense to them? This is not to say that they have to agree, often they will not. Such discussions can help you understand whether you have been silent about, or simply missed, an important issue.

You need to give readers access to both the processes and findings and, most importantly, examples of the materials that you based your analysis on.

The other crisis I referred to above, *the crisis of representation*, is intimately related to how you need to demonstrate that your account is plausible. As we analyze how talk or texts work to produce convincing arguments, we should also think about how our own research reports and presentations work to produce a specific version of the real. Researchers have argued that we need *a more explicit and reflexive stance to the ways we produce our own knowledge and academic texts*. Reports of research no longer only have to take on the form or genre of the 'typical' academic article – with introduction, literature review, methodology, and so on – where the author is hidden, where the ethical and political problems and dilemmas you faced are silenced. Some researchers present their research through various 'new literary forms', like poems, literature, drama, diaries, as well as things like dialogues embedded in the text. These dialogues are often between the author and an imaginary 'other' and can work to discuss some of the opposing perspectives or comment on the assumptions of the author's arguments. Such work reminds us all about the taken-for-granted ways we as academics construct our own arguments, it works to challenge our own assumptions about how we write, about how we make knowledge. And you could easily do some work on just how this book works to persuade you about the things it discusses.

As with nearly everything I have discussed in this book, there are no right or wrong answers to these problems. The best advice I can offer is that as you generate materials for your archive, as you produce a transcript to that level of detail, as you decide to ignore that discussion in a text you have just found, as you write up the results of your research study, be reflexive about your own practices, critically reflect on how you have rendered a specific version of the world.

Steps and key points of analyzing conversations, discourse and documents

I want to end this chapter by offering some things you may want to consider when you study conversations, discourse and documents. This is in no way meant to be a list of things you have to or should do, but rather a set of practical actions that you *may* find useful to work with.

1. *Formulate your **initial** research questions.* Your research questions may be subject to change over the course of your research.
2. *Start a research diary.* Routinely make notes of all your courses of action and (analytic) thoughts over the entire period of the research.
3. *Find possible sources of material and begin to generate an archive.* This material will be obtained by gathering pre-existing material (documents, audiotapes or videos) and/or generating the material yourself through recording interactions (audiotapes or videos). Part of your archive will also be material obtained from academic sources as well as other 'non-academic' discussions (e.g. notes on a radio programme) of topics in your research.
4. *Transcribe the texts in some detail.* The level of detail will depend on your analytic interests. If you have a very large archive, (at the very least) transcribe part of your archive. Some texts, especially documents, may not require any transcription.
5. *Sceptically read and interrogate the texts.* Re-read the texts, re-play your audio or video recordings. You should 'know your archive' better than anyone else.
6. *Code.* In the initial stages be as inclusive as possible. Do not worry if you have overlapping codes. Then use the constant comparison method to develop a comprehensive and systematic coding scheme. You will (repeatedly) revise your coding scheme as you engage with your archive.
7. *Analyze* through (a) examining regularity and variability in the data and (b) forming tentative findings. You will never be able to do detailed analysis on

everything you find. Remember that you can repeatedly go back to your archive to follow up things you did not have time to investigate previously.

8. *Check 'validity' and rigour* through (a) deviant case analysis, (b) comparing your findings to previous work and (c) showing other people your data and discussing your findings with them. These 'other people' will generally be your academic peers or supervisors but they may also be your research participants.

9. *Write up*. Reflect on your own analysis and writing practices. (Source: Based on Gill, 2000.)

Some (final) closing comments

In and through the study of conversations, discourse and documents, you can begin to re-engage with a diverse array of things, topics or ideas that you or others may take for granted. You can begin to look in wonder (and sometimes horror) at the bizarre and wonderful ways we produce social life. You can work to re-describe the encounters or texts you engage with, you can work to criticize (or celebrate) contemporary practices, and you can offer alternative ways of understanding our contemporary problems and dilemmas. In saying all this, I want to stress that this work is deeply fascinating and, above all, fun.

Further reading

These works explore more deeply the issues of quality in qualitative research:

Flick, U. (2007b) *Managing Quality in Qualitative Research* (Book 8 of *The SAGE Qualitative Research Kit*). London: Sage.
Peräkylä, A. (2004) 'Reliability and validity in research based on transcripts', in D. Silverman (ed.), *Qualitative Research: Theory, Method and Practice* (2nd edn). London: Sage, pp. 201–19.
Seale, C. (1999) *The Quality of Qualitative Research*. London: Sage.
Taylor, S. (2001b) 'Evaluating and applying discourse analytic research' in M. Wetherell, S. Taylor and S.J. Yates (eds), *Discourse as Data: A Guide for Analysis*. London: Sage, in association with The Open University, pp. 311–30.

‖ Glosssary

Archive   A diverse collection of materials that enable you to engage with and think about the specific research problem or questions. Your archive could contain document-based sources and audio- and visual-based sources as well as key research articles, notes to yourself, in fact anything that could help your analysis.

Conversation analysis   People undertaking conversation analysis focus on how social actions and practices are accomplished in and through talk and interaction. They often focus on features of interaction like: how speakers take turns at talk; how talk is shaped by prior actions and shapes what follows it; how talk is designed to perform certain actions; what words people use; and how the broader trajectory of talk is organized. The central sources of these observations are audio and video recordings of 'naturally occurring' talk and interaction.

Discourse analysis   People studying discourse are interested in how language is used in certain contexts. The focus is on how specific identities, practices, knowledge or meanings are produced by describing something in just that way over another way. This can mean a focus on language used in specific instances of interaction, like children playing, or a number of texts on a specific issue, like newspaper reports of a disaster, to a broader, often historical, focus on systems of knowledge, like the medicalization of attention deficit hyperactivity disorder.

Discursive psychology   This often draws on elements of conversation analysis, discourse analysis and rhetoric to focus on how apparently 'internal' psychological events, like 'memory', 'emotion' or 'attitudes', are produced, negotiated and accomplished in and through social actions, interactions and texts.

Naturally occurring data   Some people divide data into researcher-led or researcher-prompted – things like interviews or focus groups – and naturally occurring data – things like audiotapes of family meal-time conversations or videotapes of consultations with doctors – which would have occurred without the researcher's presence or actions. However, what I take a focus on naturally occurring data to mean is that you should use data to try to discover how some activity or interaction, be it a consultation or a qualitative interview, occurs as 'natural', normal or routine. In this sense, any data can be treated as 'naturally occurring'.

Reflexivity   As we analyze how talk or texts work to produce convincing arguments, we should also think about how our own research reports and presentations work to produce a specific version of the real. Researchers have argued that we need a more explicit and self-reflective stance to the ways we produce our own knowledge and academic texts.

Rhetoric   When studying rhetoric you are interested in how a speaker, document or text seeks to convey or consolidate a particular meaning above others whilst countering other possible meanings. You might focus on how the discourse is used to persuade you about the authority of its position and how it works to silence other possible readings.

Social constructionism   This paradigm assumes that language is never a neutral, transparent, means of communication. Put simply, our under-standing of things, concepts or ideas that we might take for granted, like 'childhood', 'evidence' or 'motive', is not somehow natural or pre-given but rather a product of human actions and interactions, history, society and culture.

Texts   The term refers to the whole range of written and visual documents that we read, use and engage with as part of our everyday lives. It can also refer to objects like trainers, or events like football matches, or other things like food, or walking styles.

Transcription   The process of transforming audio- or video-based materials into some form of written text. The most common form of transcription is to produce verbatim transcripts, where you try to document the words that were spoken alongside who spoke them. They can also include various interactional features of talk, such as pauses, laughter and overlapping, as well as details of gestures, gaze or use of objects. Transcripts are by their very nature translations; they are always partial and selective textual repre-sentations. The actual process of making detailed transcripts enables you to become familiar with what you are observing.

▐▌ References

Aalto, M. and Seppa, K. (2001) 'At which drinking level to advise a patient? General practitioners' views', *Alcohol*, 36: 431–3.

Adams, P.J., Powell, A., McCormick, R. and Paton-Simpson, G. (1997) 'Incentives for general practitioners to provide brief interventions for alcohol problems', *N.Z. Medical Journal*, 110: 291–4.

Allistone, S. (2002) 'A conversation analytic study of parents' evening', unpublished PhD dissertation, Goldsmiths' College, University of London.

Angrosino, M. (2007) *Doing Ethnographic and Observational Research* (Book 3 of *The SAGE Qualitative Research Kit*). London: Sage.

Antaki, C. (2002) *An Introductory Tutorial in Conversation Analysis*. Online at http://www-staff.lboro.ac.uk/~sscal/sitemenu.htm; accessed on 5 Oct. 2005.

Arminen, I. (2000) 'On the context sensitivity of institutional interaction', *Discourse and Society*, 11: 435–58.

Ashmore, M. and Reed, D. (2000) 'Innocence and nostalgia in conversation analysis: the dynamic relations of tape and transcript', *Forum Qualitative Sozialforschung/Forum: Qualitative Social Research* (Online Journal), 1(3). Online at http://www.qualitative-research.net/fqs-texte/3-00/3-00ashmorereed-e.htm accessed on 12 Jan. 2006.

Asthana, A. and Doward, D. (2003) 'Binge drinking: do they mean us?', *The Observer*, Sunday 21 Dec.

Babor, T.F., Ritson, B.E. and Hodgson, R.J. (1986) 'Alcohol-related problems in the primary health care setting: a review of early intervention strategies', *British Journal of Addiction*, 81: 23–46.

Balint, M. (1955) 'The doctor, his patient and the illness', The *Lancet*, i: 683–8.

Banks, M. (2007) *Using Visual Data in Qualitative Research* (Book 5 of *The SAGE Qualitative Research Kit*). London: Sage.

Barbour, R. (2007) *Doing Focus Groups* (Book 4 of *The SAGE Qualitative Research Kit*). London: Sage.

Beach, W.A. and Metzinger, T.R. (1997) 'Claiming insufficient knowledge', *Human Communication Research*, 23(4): 562–88.

Billig, M. (1999) 'Whose terms? Whose ordinariness? Rhetoric and ideology in conversation analysis', *Discourse and Society*, 10(4): 543–58.

Branley, D. (2004) 'Making and managing audio recordings', in C. Seale (ed.), *Researching Society and Culture* (2nd edn). London: Sage, pp. 207–24.

Burr, V. (1995) *An Introduction to Social Constructionism*. London: Routledge.

Davidson, J. (1984) 'Subsequent versions of invitations, offers, requests and proposals dealing with potential or actual rejection', in J.M. Atkinson and J. Heritage (eds), *Structures of Social Action: Studies in Conversational Analysis*. Cambridge: Cambridge University Press, pp. 102–28.

References

Denzin, N. (1988) 'Qualitative analysis for social scientists', *Contemporary Sociology*, 17: 430–2.

Drew, P. (1984) 'Speakers' reportings in invitation sequences', in J.M. Atkinson and J. Heritage (eds), *Structures of Social Action: Studies in Conversational Analysis*. Cambridge: Cambridge University Press, pp. 129–51.

Drew, P. (1992) 'Contested evidence in courtroom cross-examination: the case of a trial for rape', in P. Drew and J. Heritage (eds), *Talk at Work: Interaction in Institutional Settings*. Cambridge: Cambridge University Press, pp. 470–520.

Drew, P. and Heritage, J. (1992) 'Analyzing talk at work: an introduction', in P. Drew and J. Heritage (eds), *Talk at Work: Interaction in Institutional Settings*. Cambridge: Cambridge University Press, pp. 3–65.

Economic and Social Research Council (2005) *ESRC Research Ethics Framework*. Online at http://www.esrc.ac.uk/ref; accessed on 21 Feb. 2006.

Edley, N. (2001) 'Analysing masculinity: interpretative repertoires, ideological dilemmas and subject positions', in M. Wetherell, S. Taylor and S.J. Yates (eds), *Discourse as Data: A Guide to Analysis*. London: Sage, in association with the Open University, pp. 189–228.

Edley, N. and Wetherell, M. (1997) 'Jockeying for position: the construction of masculine identities', *Discourse and Society*, 8: 203–17.

Emerson, R.M. (2004) 'Working with "key incidents"' in C. Seale, G. Gobo, J.F. Gubrium and D. Silverman (eds), *Qualitative Research Practice*. London: Sage, pp. 457–72.

Firth, H. and Kitzinger, C. (1998) '"Emotion work" as a participant's resource: a feminist analysis of young women's talk in interaction', *Sociology*, 32(2): 299–320.

Flick, U. (2007a) *Designing Qualitative Research* (Book 1 of *The SAGE Qualitative Research Kit*). London: Sage.

Flick, U. (2007b) *Managing Quality in Qualitative Research* (Book 8 of *The SAGE Qualitative Research Kit*). London: Sage.

Garfinkel, H. (1967) *Studies in Ethnomethodology*. Englewood Cliffs, NJ: Prentice-Hall.

General Medical Council (2002) *Making and Using Visual and Audio Recordings of Patients*, http://www.gmc-uk.org/stantards/AUD_VID.HTM.

Gibbs, G. (2007) *Analyzing Qualitative Data* (Book 6 of *The SAGE Qualitative Research Kit*). London: Sage.

Gidley, B. (2003) 'Citizenship and belonging: East London Jewish Radicals 1903–1918, unpublished PhD dissertation, Goldsmiths' College, University of London.

Gidley, B. (2004) 'Doing historical and archival research', in C. Seale (ed.), *Researching Society and Culture* (2nd edn). London: Sage, pp. 249–64.

Gill, R. (2000) 'Discourse analysis', in M.W. Bauer and G. Gaskell (eds), *Qualitative Researching with Text, Image and Sound*. London: Sage, pp. 172–90.

Glaser, B.G. (1965) 'The constant comparative method of qualitative analysis', *Social Problems*, 12: 436–45.

Goodwin, C. (1994a) 'Professional vision', *American Anthropologist*, 96(3): 606–33.

Goodwin, C. (1994b) 'Recording human interaction in natural settings', *Pragmatics*, 3(2): 181–209.

Gothill, M. and Armstrong, D. (1999) 'Dr No-body: the construction of the doctor as an embodied subject in British general practice 1955–1997', *Sociology of Health and Illness*, 21: 1–12.

Hak, T. (1992) 'Psychiatric records as transformations of other texts' in G. Watson and R.M. Seiler (eds), *Text in Context: Contributions to Ethnomethodology*. Newbury Park, CA: Sage, pp. 138–55.

Hak, T. (1998) '"There are clear delusions": the production of a factual account', *Human Studies*, 21: 419–36.

Hall, S. (2002) 'New wave of "sophisticated" alcopops fuels teenage binge drinking', *The Guardian*, Saturday 14 Dec.

References

Hepburn, A. and Potter, J. (2003). 'Discourse analytic practice', in C. Seale, D. Silverman, J. Gubrium and G. Gobo (eds), *Qualitative Research Practice*. London: Sage, pp. 180–96.

Heritage, J. (1984) *Garfinkel and Ethnomethodology*. Cambridge: Polity Press.

Heritage, J. (1997) 'Conversation analysis and institutional talk: analysing data', in D. Silverman (ed.), *Qualitative Research: Theory, Method and Practice*. London: Sage, pp. 222–45.

Heritage, J. and Greatbatch, D. (1991) 'On the institutional character of institutional talk: the case of news interviews', in D. Boden and D.H. Zimmerman (eds), *Talk and Social Structure: Studies in Ethnomethodology and Conversation Analysis*. Berkeley: University of California Press, pp. 93–137.

Holstein, J.A. and Gubrium, J.F. (1995) *The Active Interview*. Thousand Oaks, CA: Sage.

Hutchby, I. (1996) *Confrontation Talk: Arguments, Asymmetries, and Power on Talk Radio*. Mahwah, NJ: Lawrence Erlbaum.

Jefferson, G. (2004) 'Glossary of transcript symbols with an introduction', in C.H. Lerner (ed.) *Conversation Analysis: Studies from the First Generation*. Philadelphia: John Benjamins, pp. 13–23.

Jenkings, K.N. and Barber, N. (2004) 'What constitutes evidence in hospital new drug decision making?', *Social Science and Medicine*, 58: 1757–66.

Jenkings, K.N. and Barber, N. (2006) 'Same evidence, different meanings: transformation of textual evidence in hospital new drugs committees' *Text and Talk*, 26(2): 169–89.

Kelly, M. and Ali, S. (2004) 'Ethics and social research', in C. Seale (ed.), *Researching Society and Culture* (2nd edn). London: Sage, pp. 115–28.

Kitzinger, C. and Firth, H. (1999) '"Just say no?" The use of conversation analysis in developing a feminist perspective on sexual refusal', *Discourse and Society*, 10(3): 293–316.

Kvale, S. (2007) *Doing Interviews* (Book 2 of *The SAGE Qualitative Research Kit*). London: Sage.

Lee, J. (1984) 'Innocent victims and evil-doers', *Women's Studies International Forum*, 7: 69–73.

Livingston, E. (1987) *Making Sense of Ethnomethodology*. London: Routledge & Kegan Paul, chap. 15.

Lynch, M. (1993) *Scientific Practice and Ordinary Action*. Cambridge: Cambridge University Press.

May, C.R. (1997) 'Pathology, identity and the social construction of alcohol dependence', *Sociology*, 35: 385–401.

Maynard, D.W. (1991) 'On the interactional and institutional basis of asymmetry in clinical discourse', *American Journal of Sociology*, 92(2): 488–95.

Maynard, D.W. (1992) 'On clinicians co-implicating recipients' perspective in the delivery of diagnostic news', in P. Drew and J. Heritage (eds), *Talk at Work: Interaction in Institutional Settings*. Cambridge: Cambridge University Press, pp. 331–58.

Moerman, M. (1988) *Talking Culture: Ethnography and Conversation Analysis*. Philadelphia: University of Pennsylvania Press.

Moerman, M. (1992) 'Life after C.A.', in G. Watson and R.M. Seiler (eds), *Text in Context: Contributions to Ethnomethodology*. New York: Sage, pp. 20–34.

Newcastle Herald and Post (2004) 'Herald and Post Meeting Place', Wednesday 4 Aug.

Peräkylä, A. (2004) 'Reliability and validity in research based on transcripts', in D. Silverman, *Qualitative Research: Theory, Method and Practice* (2nd edn). London: Sage, pp. 201–19.

Poland, B.D. (2002) 'Transcription quality', in J. Gubrium and J. Holstein (eds), *Handbook of Interview Research: Context and Method*. Thousand Oaks, CA: Sage, pp. 629–50.

References

Pomerantz, A. (1984) 'Agreeing and disagreeing with assessments: some features of preferred/dispreferred turn shapes', in J.M. Atkinson and J. Heritage (eds), *Structures of Social Action: Studies in Conversation Analysis*. Cambridge: Cambridge University Press, pp. 57–101.

Potter, J. (1996a) 'Discourse analysis and constructionist approaches: theoretical background', in J. Richardson (ed.), *Handbook of Qualitative Research Methods for Psychology and the Social Sciences*. Leicester: BPS, pp. 125–40.

Potter, J. (1996b) *Representing Reality: Discourse, Rhetoric and Social Construction*. London: Sage.

Potter, J. (1997) 'Discourse analysis as a way of analysing naturally occurring talk', in D. Silverman (ed.), *Qualitative Research: Theory, Method and Practice*. London: Sage, pp. 200–20.

Prior, L. (2003) *Using Documents in Social Research*. London: Sage.

Rose, N. (1998) 'Life, reason and history: reading Georges Canguilhem today', *Economy and Society*, 27(2–3): 154–70.

Rubin, H.J. and Rubin, I.S. (1995) *Qualitative Interviewing; The Art of Hearing Data*. Thousand Oaks, CA: Sage.

Ryan, A. (2005) 'Ethical issues', in C. Seale, G. Gobo., J.F. Gubrium and D. Silverman (eds), *Qualitative Research Practice*. London: Sage, pp. 230–47.

Sacks, H. (1984) 'Notes on methodology', in J.M. Atkinson and J. Heritage (eds), *Structures of Social Action: Studies in Conversation Analysis*. Cambridge: Cambridge University Press, pp. 21–7.

Sacks, H. (1995) *Lectures on Conversation*. Oxford: Blackwell.

Schegloff, E.A. (1999) 'Discourse, pragmatics, conversation, analysis', *Discourse Studies*, 1(4): 405–35.

Schegloff, M. (1997) 'Whose text? Whose context?', *Discourse and Society*, 8: 165–87.

Scott, J. (1990) *A Matter of Record: Documentary Sources in Social Research*. Cambridge: Polity Press.

Seale, C. (1999) *The Quality of Qualitative Research*. London: Sage.

Seale, C. (2002) 'Cancer heroics: a study of news reports with particular reference to gender', *Sociology*, 36: 107–26.

Silverman, D. (1987) *Communication and Medical Practice*. London: Sage.

Silverman, D. (1998) *Harvey Sacks: Social Science and Conversation Analysis*. Cambridge: Polity Press.

Smith, D.E. (1990) *Texts, Facts and Femininity: Exploring the Relations of Ruling*. London: Routledge.

Strong, P.M. (1980) 'Doctors and dirty work – the case of alcoholism', *Sociology of Health and Illness*, 2: 24–47.

Taylor, S. (2001a) 'Locating and conducting discourse analytic research', in M. Wetherell, S. Taylor and S.J. Yates (eds) *Discourse as Data: A Guide for Analysis*. London: Sage, in association with The Open University, pp. 5–48.

Taylor, S. (2001b) 'Evaluating and applying discourse analytic research', in M. Wetherell, S. Taylor and S.J. Yates (eds), *Discourse as Data: A Guide for Analysis*. London: Sage, in association with The Open University, pp. 311–30.

ten Have, P (1999) *Doing Conversation Analysis: A Practical Guide*. London: Sage.

van Dijk, T.A. (1999) 'Critical discourse analysis and conversation analysis', *Discourse and Society*, 9(3): 459–60.

von Lehm, D., Heath, C. and Hindmarsh, J. (2001) 'Exhibiting interaction: conduct and collaboration in museums and galleries', *Symbolic Interaction*, 24: 189–216.

Wetherell, M. (1998) 'Positioning and interpretative repertoires: conversation analysis and post-structuralism in dialogue', *Discourse and Society*, 9: 387–412.

References

Wetherell, M. (2001) 'Themes in discourse research: the case of Diana', in M. Wetherell, S. Taylor and S.J. Yates (eds), *Discourse Theory and Practice: A Reader*. London: Sage, in association with The Open University, pp. 14–28.

Wetherell, M., Taylor, S. and Yates, S.J. (eds), *Discourse Theory and Practice: A Reader*. London: Sage, in association with The Open University.

Williams, C., Kitzinger, J. and Henderson, H. (2003) 'Envisaging the embryo in stem cell research: rhetorical strategies and media reporting of the ethical debates', *Sociology of Health and Illness*, 25: 793–814.

▌▌▌ Author index

III Subject index